A MESSIANIC COMMENTARY

*Yeshua's Brother & Chief Rabbi of
the Messianic Jewish Community*

JAMES THE JUST
YA'AKOV HATZADDIK

PRESENTS
APPLICATIONS OF TORAH

ENDORSEMENTS

David Friedman does it again. After enlig   me in his work on
Bereshit, he gives me a whole new perspect   ow to view the book
of Ya'acov. With his scholarship and kno   of ancient Hebrew
texts, Dr. Friedman puts Ya'acov back into las correct historical context
and gives us much to chew on. His work sho ld be read by any serious
student of the Brit Chadasha with an open mi d.

   --Dr. M. Leibowitz, Tempe, AZ

Dr. David Friedman has written a fascinating work on the letter of
Ya'akov- James, the Messianic Chief Rabbi of the time; a Yalkut –
collection of instructive interpretation of the book of Leviticus. The
Yalkut was a work in *"halakha ma'asit"*, a very practical development
and application of the commandments of the Torah. Ya'akov wrote
and explained to his community how they were to walk and follow
the Derech – The Way of the Torah as a Jewish community of Yeshua
Followers. Friedman takes the reader back to the culture, community,
and context which were all thoroughly Jewish. By examining the Greek
texts and their word structures, he brings out the hidden Jewish concepts
in this practical manual for Jewish life.

   – S.H.R. ben Haim, MILIM-MJTI Center, Jerusalem, Israel.

The book of James has often been a lightening rod of controversy
for New Testament scholars. Ironically, many have misunderstood
important themes of the book because they were unaware of first century
Jewish literature genres.
   Dr. David Friedman's latest work does much to place the scroll back
in its original Jewish context and thus enlightens the reader with fresh
insight into our walk with Messiah Yeshua.

   --Rabbi Barney Kasdan, Kehilat Ariel Messianic Synagogue, San
   Diego, CA and author of Matthew Presents Yeshua, King Messiah

Dr. David Friedman is a man that I often refer to as a "Scholar and a Gentleman." It is a privilege to once again drink from his deep well of knowledge and understanding of the ancient languages of Scripture. It is the desire of every serious student of the Bible to know the original meanings of words and to gain an understanding of the proper context in which the letter of James was written.

--Pastor Steven Shelley, Salem, AL.

Dr. Friedman's analysis of the book of James is insightful in a way that is unique from any commentary I have seen on the subject. What is unique about Dr. Friedman's commentary is that he draws the reader into a deep contextualization of the book in the milieu of first century Judaism. I'd like to be first in line for the completed work!

--Rabbi Charlie Cohen, Congregation Tsemach Adonai, Los Gatos, California; Treasurer, Union of Messianic Jewish Congregations

Dr. David Friedman has written a refreshing look at the book of James/ Ya'acov, making it clearly understood that there is a balance of Torah observance and God's grace. David's distinctive writing makes it obvious to the reader to become motivated in adherence to Torah. This book will enhance our understanding of the spirit of Torah, our teaching, and the living out of the whole of the Devar/Word.

--Shmuel Oppenheim, Rabbi, Lev HaShem Messianic Jewish Synagogue, Las Vegas, Nevada

Dr. Friedman has struck a chord. Placing James in his native Hebraic context brings clarity and understanding to New Testament scholarship, which has generally considered Torah commandments "old" theology and obsolete. If Yeshua did not abolish the Torah (Matthew 5:17), then what of the Torah are we to keep? David Friedman sheds new light on this old question. I gained new insight into one of my favorite books of the Bible.

--Hylan Slobodkin, Messianic Rabbi, Beit Tikvah Messianic Congregation, Newcastle, WA

A MESSIANIC COMMENTARY

*Yeshua's Brother & Chief Rabbi of
the Messianic Jewish Community*

JAMES THE JUST
YA'AKOV HATZADDIK

PRESENTS
APPLICATIONS OF TORAH

DAVID FRIEDMAN
with
B. D. FRIEDMAN

Lederer Books
A division of
Messianic Jewish Publishers
Clarksville, MD 21029

Scripture quotations are taken from the Complete Jewish Bibl   pyright
©1998 by David H. Stern, published by Jewish New Testament F   ations,
Inc.; New International Version, copyright ©1984, International Bil   ociety;
and from Bereshit: The Book of Beginnings, by David Friedmaᵤ   ᵤyright
©2010, Wipf and Stock. Hebrew quotations are taken from the Qoreᵤ   lishers
Tanakh.

15 14 13 12   6 5 4 3 2

Library of Congress Control Number: 2012941580
ISBN 978-1-936716-44-9
Printed in the United States of America
Copyright © 2012 by David Friedman, Ph.D.
with
B. D. Friedman

Published by
Lederer Books
A division of
Messianic Jewish Publishers
6120 Day Long Lane
Clarksville, Maryland 21029

Distributed by
Messianic Jewish Resources Int'l.
www.messianicjewish.net
Individual and Trade Order line: 800-410-7367

Email: lederer@messianicjewish.net

To Micah

May you grow to be a tree planted by water streams, that sends out its roots by the stream (Jeremiah 17.8).

"The very world rests on the breath of a child in the schoolhouse." (Talmud Bavli: Shabbat, 119b).

May you grow to be the person that you were created to be: full of life and joy.

CONTENTS

TABLES

GENERAL EDITOR'S PREFACE

Nearly all bible commentators emphasize the importance of understanding the historical, cultural and grammatical aspects of any text of scripture. As has been said, "A text without a context is a pretext." In other words, to assume one can understand what God has revealed through those who present his word—prophets, poets, visionaries, apostles— without knowing the context is presumption. To really understand God's word, it's essential to know something about who wrote it and to whom, what was actually said and what it originally meant, when, where, and why it was written.

By now, everyone knows that the New Testament is a thoroughly Jewish book, written nearly entirely by Jews, taking place in and around Israel. The people written about—Paul, Peter, James, John, etc.—were almost all Jews who never abandoned their identities or people. The topics covered—sin, salvation, resurrection, Torah, Sabbath, how to "walk with God," the Millennium, etc.—were all Jewish topics that came from the Hebrew scripture. The expressions used often were Jewish idioms of that day. So, to fully understand the New Testament, it must be viewed through "Jewish eyes," meaning that the Jewish historical, cultural, grammatical must be examined.

There are commentaries for women, for men, for teens, even for children. There are commentaries that focus on financial issues in the bible. Others provide archaeological material. Some commentaries are topical. Others are the works of eminent men and women of God. But, until now, no commentary series has closely looked at the Jewish context of the New Testament books.

In this series, we have invited some of the top Messianic Jewish theologians in the world to contribute their knowledge and understanding. Each has written on a book (or more) of the New Testament they've specialized in, making sure to present the Jewish aspects—the original context—of each book. These works are not meant to be a verse-by-verse exegetical commentary. There are already many excellent ones available. But, these commentaries supplement what others lack, by virtue of the fact they were not focusing on the Jewish aspects.

A number of different authors wrote these commentaries, each in his own style. Just as the Gospels were written by four different men, each with his own perspective and style, these volumes, too, have variations. We didn't want the writers to have to conform too much to any particular style guide, other than our basic one.

You may see some use the Hebrew transliteration of the names in the New Testament. Thus, one writer might refer to the Apostle to the Gentiles as Paul. Another might write, Shaul, Paul's Hebrew name. Still, another might write Saul, an

Anglicized version of Shaul. And some might write Saul/Paul, to reflect the different ways this servant of Messiah was known.

Another variation is the amount of reference material. Some have ample footnotes or endnotes, while others incorporate references within the text. Some don't have an enormous amounts of notes, based on the book they are writing commentary for.

We have plans for a Messianic Jewish commentary series on the entire bible. Although much has been written on the books of the Hebrew Scriptures, and there have been some written by Messianic Jews, there hasn't been a full commentary series on the "Older" Testament. But, we hope to publish such a series in the near future.

So, I invite you to put on your Jewish glasses (if you're not Jewish) and take a look at the New Testament in a way that will truly open up new understanding for you, as you get to know the God of Israel and his Messiah better.

Rabbi Baruch Rubin
General Editor

FOREWORD

A Messianic Commentary of Ya'akov (James)

Ya'akov (James) has always been one of my favourite books in the B'rit Hadasha and the content has always resonated in my spirit. Many of the verses from this book are the ones I quote frequently in my teachings, as they were relevant to my life and walk with HaShem.

After listening to Rabbi David Friedman, I realized that the resonance in my spirit was because these verses were penned by a Jewish rabbi teaching Torah to his students and to the messianic Jews living in the Diaspora. The foundation was thoroughly Jewish! Although clothed in Greek and lost in translation in the English, Rabbi David asserted that the foundations in Torah were present and he proceeded to uncover them.

Rabbi David Friedman makes several proposals concerning Rabbi Ya'akov: That the writings of Ya'akov were a specific style of rabbinic writings, a collection if you will of a particular rabbi's sayings and teachings (in

Hebrew a Yalkut), collated by his talmidim (disciples) and disseminated to a wider audience in the dispersion. He points out that the purpose of his writings was to instruct the Messianic Jewish community in Israel and beyond it's borders on how to practically apply Torah in the context of their daily lives in that milieu. Rabbi Friedman states that Ya'akov's writings were a commentary on the book of Leviticus, specifically chapters 19:1 to the middle of chapter 20 (Parshat Kedoshim). He also examines how Ya'akov's writings represented the collected highlights of his teaching and commentaries and was memorized by his talmidim for the purpose of disseminating to a wider audience.

Many Hebrew idioms contained in Ya'akov's writings are 'lost in translation.' In most of the English translations, one can easily read all five chapters without discovering its connection to Torah.

I've alluded to just a handful of such illustrations:

In James 1:1 the intended audience is clearly identified: *"to the twelve tribes in the Diaspora."* So we know that his audience is the messianic Jewish community living outside the Land. 1:27 *" ... care for orphans and widows in their distress,"* is common to many societies, but Torah teaches communal responsibility for the defenseless, the orphan and the widow: *Deut 27:19 'Cursed is the one who perverts the justice due the stranger, the fatherless, and widow.' And all the people shall say, "Amen!"* And looking at 4:5 – *'Or do you suppose the Scripture speaks in vain when it says that there is a spirit in us which longs to envy?* [1] Scripture must refer to Torah, for there were no scriptures in the Greek world. Lev 19:18 is a clear reference to the inclination to envy and its consequences.

It requires some effort to reread Ya'akov through a Hebraic lens but it will undoubtedly enrich your understanding of the Word of God. Having tasted a mere morsel, I look forward with anticipation to Rabbi Friedman's book on this topic.

Herschel Raysman
Congregational Leader, Beit Ariel, Cape Town, South Africa

INTRODUCTION

Three important questions we will ask:
1. Who was Ya'akov?
2. Is this book a "rabbinic yalkut"?
3. What are the main points of the book, the "yalkut"?

"Yalkut": a collection of highlighted teachings by a rabbi, often collected by his students.

Main emphases of the yalkut:
- "halakha ma'asit" [practical Torah]
- practical encouragement on how to live
- not philosophical, but concrete: instructional guides on how to live according to Torah
- most misunderstood point: "faith & works." Ya'akov's point: keeping the instructions of the Torah is proof that one has strong faith in God and in Messiah Yeshua.

The book of James was a collection of highlights from the sermons of the chief rabbi of Jerusalem's Messianic Jewish community. I surmise that James gave these sermon talks on Sabbaths during which the ending section of the book of Leviticus was being studied.

1

As James (Ya'akov was his real name) was functioning as the chief rabbi of his early Messianic Jewish community centered in Jerusalem, his role would have been that of Torah teacher par excellence, chief halakhic judge and authority, and spokesman for the entire community.[1] The books of Acts and James record Ya'akov as active in all three roles. Ya'akov was probably the brother of Yeshua the Messiah, and was picked for his all-important role due to a variety of reasons. In fact, it is recorded by Eusebius, the 4th century historian-bishop, that the first few chief rabbis of the early flagship Messianic Jewish community were descendants of Yeshua's wider family. [2] When we view Ya'akov for who he was: a chief rabbi, a Torah scholar, a Bible commentator, and akin to a high court judge, then we can better understand the purpose of his book.

The subjects that are taken up in James are the same ones that are taken up in Leviticus 19-22, which today constitute a single Sabbath reading that is done each year in late winter. These subjects include the proper use of speech (termed in rabbinic literature the laws of "*lashon ha-ra, sarah, dibah*" and "*hotse'et shem ra*", that is, the laws of "improper speech, speaking behind someone's back, smearing another" and "slander").

Ya'akov expounds upon more subjects found in Leviticus 19-22. These include: proper business practices, contractual oaths, the showing of favoritism in legal matters, the value of being humble, society's obligation to widows and orphans, and finally, the "royal law" of the Torah. Logically, we can assume that Ya'akov was teaching about this portion of the Torah when his words were written down by a scribe or by his students, for distribution into the Diaspora as instructional guides for communities. Alternatively, his "book" may have been distributed and studied as commentary to Leviticus 19-22 in early Messianic Jewish communities in the Diaspora.

Its Diaspora audience (see James 1.1) is the reason that Ya'akov's words were recorded in Greek. This was the lingua franca of Jews in the Mediterranean world of the first century, which included communities living in Egypt, in Syria, in Lebanon, in Turkey, in Cyprus and in Greece. These Jewish communities read and spoken Greek. It is certain that Ya'akov taught in Mishnaic Hebrew, his native tongue, though he may have been fluent in Aramaic. There is no doubt that he could have had some knowledge of Greek.

Yet, behind the Koine Greek of the letter of James are thoroughly Torah-based concepts. This is not a Hellenist work of philosophy or religion. It is Jewish in subject matter, tone, emphasis and in its main expressed points. The textual sources for the subject matters of Ya'akov's book are all from the five books of Moses. Jewish communities of his time regularly discussed the subject matters that he teaches about, and the very scriptures that he quotes. He does not present us with new teaching, but with a uniquely Messianic Jewish view of Torah-based concepts.

One of the main thrusts of Ya'akov's teaching is encouraging "*asiyat hatorah*" (that is, the practical application of the Torah's teachings). Ya'akov brilliantly states:

> Don't deceive yourselves by only hearing what the Word says, but do it! For whoever hears the Word but doesn't do what it says is like someone who looks at his face in a mirror, who looks at

3

himself, goes away and immediately f ret vhat
he looks like. But if a person looks clo in the
perfect *Torah*, which gives freedom, an ntinues,
becoming not a forgetful hearer but a er f the
work it requires, then he will be blessed in v it he
does. (James 1.22-25, CJB).

An outstanding rabbi in the first century was the son of
Paul's teacher, Gamliel. His name was Shimon, and he taught:
"...the most important matter is not study (of the Torah), but
its practice" (Pirke Avot 1.17, author's translation). Ya'akov
and Shimon were teaching the same perspective on this
subject. The student of the book of James will want to keep this
emphasis on "*asiyat hatorah*" in mind as a general conceptual
framework from which to understand this book.

It is also crucial for the student of the Bible to see the
continuity between the teachings of Ya'akov and Paul. An
incorrect understanding of Ya'akov's writings on "faith and
works" too often leads a student to view Ya'akov and Shaul
as diametrically opposed to each other concerning the role
of faith, and on the function of "works". In reading James,
we should view the term "works" as the performance of the
biblical commandments. This is how the first century Jewish
world defined this concept of "works". All first century Jews,
including Messianic Jews, saw the performance of the biblical
commandments as stemming *from* one's faith in God, *never*
in opposition to it. Secondly, in Jewish thought, the purpose
of fulfilling the biblical commandments *never* was to earn
entrance into the world to come. That is a huge misconception
of students of the New Testament.

4

To summarize, the student of this book should hear Ya'akov from his role as Torah teacher and chief rabbi who expounded on the proper keeping of the Torah. If we understand Ya'akov's belief that faith in God and in His Messiah is the base for proper fulfilling of the biblical commandments, then his book makes good sense conceptually. Alleged contradictions fall away, and it can then be studied as a community instructional guide and Bible commentary par excellence.

EXPLANATION OF HOW THE OLD TESTAMENT DESIGNATION "YA'AKOV" (Hebrew) BECAME THE NEW TESTAMENT DESIGNATION, "IAKOBOY" (Greek)

(Greek - Ἰάκωβος (Iáko-vos)

John Wycliffe was an early advocate for translation of the bible into the common language. He and his associates translated directly from the Vulgate. This work was started in 1382 and completed (with revisions) in 1388. The Vulgate is a fourth century Latin translation of the bible that was commissioned to unify all other existing writings and/or translations. It seems that Mr. Wycliffe, and many others, didn't see a need to properly translate the name "Jacob" and just used the Latin interpretation. There also seems to be an attempt to distance the New Testament from any Hebrew or

Aramaic influence. When ⸳ ⸳ ⸳ as translated into Latin, the name "Iacobos" became ⸳ra⸳ ⸳rated into "Iacobus" and late Latin turned that into ⸳lac⸳ ⸳," the "b" and the "m" being somewhat similar in ⸳ou⸳ ⸳ nasal languages. The early French version of this Latin ⸳ ⸳e became the shortened "Gemmes" which then traveled ⸳ the English speaking world as James. When the bible ⸳ranslated into English, the translators shortened the Gr⸳ ⸳nes into the versions we know now: Paulos became Pau⸳l, ⸳ ⸳s became Peter; but the name Iacobos didn't become Jacob, ⸳ecame James. King James VI of Scotland had ordered in 160⸳ "a translation to be made of the whole bible, as close as possible to the original Hebrew and Greek." The name James, which comes from Jacob, comes out of the Anglo-Saxon tradition. The name Jacob, which means "a follower" follows the French/Norman tradition (Jacobin, for example). This is just another instance where man has intervened to change the truth. This situation is minor, but where else has man changed the truth of the bible? Unfortunately, in many places!

> - author anonymous – there are a number of critics to
> these statements
> http://ask.studybible.info/246/why-did-wycliffe-
> translate-άκωβος-as-james-instead-of-jacob

Chapter One

THE BACKGROUND OF THE BOOK: YALQUT, GREEK AND "THE PRINCIPAL MATTER"

‫...ולא המדרש הוא העיקר אלא המעשה.‬
"...the principal matter is not study (of the Torah),
but practice" (Pirke Avot 1.17, author's translation).

W hat I purpose to do in this essay is to suggest a
framework by which to study the book of James.
This is neither a comprehensive overview, nor based on a
thorough text analysis, which would be a very difficult task
for our given subject.

I am reminded of a flight that I once took aboard a
Lufthansa plane. While over the Atlantic, a wing of our aircraft
was struck by lightning. Our pilot immediately spoke over
the loudspeaker system with a pronounced German accent,
"Ladies and gentlemen, we have just been struck by lightning.
Nevertheless, we shall continue." The circumstances were not

ideal, but the pilot and his grateful passengers had no choice but to go on. In a similar fashion, while the formulation of a clear answer to my question, posed in the title, lacks the abundant historical and linguistic evidence to help us reach a quick conclusion under ideal circumstances. But as the pilot stated, "nevertheless we shall continue." I will examine the text and suggest an answer for our question, in light of the few textual and historic evidences that we do possess.

First, I will give my working definition of the Hebrew term יַלְקוּט (*yalqut*) as a compilation, collection or compendium of Jewish religious writings. In modern Hebrew, this word refers to a "backpack" (in which an array of books and school supplies is carried by a pupil). Thus in this essay, I use the term "yalqut" to refer to an edition of teachings by a rabbi (in this case, Ya'akov). The most famous yalqut in rabbinic literature may be the *Yalqut Shim'oni*, a collection of the commentaries of Rabbi Shimon of Frankfurt (13th century). It is available for study at this Web site: http://www.tsel.org/torah/yalqutsh/index.html.

The *Yalqut Shim'oni* is a collection of midrashic and aggadic commentary to the text of the Bible. In general, such a yalqut will be a collection of writings that explain biblical passages, most often arranged according to the order of verses in the Bible. Bakhos describes three Medieval rabbinic yalqut writings as "thesaurus-like collections…amassed rabbinic saying(s)…into a collection ordered according to the verses of the Bible…The rabbis engaged in biblical exegesis not only for the purpose of understanding the Bible, but…to make its meaning relevant to their world."[1]

Yalqut Yosef is a modern yalqut, a thirty-volume set of writings by Rabbi Ovadya Yosef, the former Chief Sephardic

10

Rabbi of Israel. It is a concentrated compilation of his writings, which instruct on how to best keep the biblical commandments and their ensuing customs in today's modern society. This neatly fits the definition of Bakhos. Another contemporary yalqut is the Yalqut Siach b'sadeh, which is a compilation of prayers, translated and edited by Rabbi Eliezer Brody.

Other historic yalqut editions include the Yalqut ha-Makhiri, Yalqut Me'am Lo'ez, Yalqut Eliezer and the Yalqut Re'uveni. Today, an edition entitled Yalqut Bar Mitzvah has been published and is an anthology of bar mitzvah customs, traditions, history, readings and possibilities. Again, this yalqut is a collection of writings that gives purpose and direction to the event of a bar mitzvah.

In terms of purpose, the book of James meets the functional definition of Bakhos for a yalqut. It, too, supplies us with a rabbi's compiled writings that, in Bakhos' words above, purpose to "instruct on how to best keep the biblical commandments" and "to make [their] meaning relevant to [his given] world." Although the book of James is from an earlier time period than the Medieval era, and its content is less in volume than extant yalqut editions, it does bear similarities to a Medieval yalqut. It, too, is a collection of a rabbi's teachings, complete with an arranged order, possibly according to *parashat Kedoshim* (see glossary). With just this much in mind, we will examine the book of James and see how it fits into this general framework.

I will argue that the above points were exactly the purpose of Ya'akov (and his students) in compiling and distributing the book of James. In the words of Bakhos, it was "to make the Torah relevant to their world." So, do we have a collection (i.e.

yalqut) of Torah exposition lessons by Ya   in his book?

As a Jewish student of the book o   m   the first few times I read this book, I was immediatei st   with a sense that I was looking at something quite Jev ich   iindset, form and content. However, these aspects sec   'most hidden and "under wraps" in English translatioi   ie book. The fact that the oldest copies of this book exist in a Greek text can promote further distancing of its contents from its very Jewish context and subject matter.

However, the existence of James in Greek, and not in a Hebrew original, is easily explained. Certainly Ya'akov delivered his talks on the Torah in his native language: Mishnaic Hebrew.[2] However, due to the fact that his teachings were going to be distributed to communities of the western Diaspora of the Jewish world, the existence of a Greek edition was crucial. As Hebrew University history professor Doron Mendels put it: "In the Hellenistic period, Jews were living all over the then-known world. Jerusalem and the Land of Israel, however, provided a central unifying force binding this extensive Jewish world together."[3] As was the case in the wider, first century Jewish Diaspora, so it was with the Messianic Jewish community. In Mendel's words above, its "central, unifying force," though not an official one, was also Jerusalem based. This fact is both logical and historically accurate. Jewish believers in the Diaspora were helped by the unifying presence of the "mother," flagship community in Jerusalem.

Much of the western Diaspora (including Jewish communities in nearby Egypt) was not fluent in Hebrew, and spoke Greek as their native language.[4] Therefore, the existence

12

of the book of James in a literary style of Greek is no surprise. In fact, the early church father Jerome claimed that Ya'akov (or perhaps more accurately, his community) employed a scribe(s) who translated his lessons into good Greek. This would have been due to the necessity for distributing his lessons to the Messianic Jewish Diaspora in the west. This was common practice in the Mediterranean world of the first century: "The Greek papyri . . . indicate quite clearly that an amanuensis was frequently, if not commonly, employed in the writing of personal letters during the time approximating the composition of the NT epistles."[5] If this is what happened with Ya'akov's teachings, then: "there is hardly any necessity for James to know Greek well; he merely needed to employ a learned scribe."[6] Any immigrant to Israel from the western Diaspora, who was one of his students or a member of the Jerusalem Messianic Jewish community, could have carried out this task. "Plenty of scribes in Jerusalem were so trained," remark Shanks and Witherington.[7]

It is of note that some commentators have discerned a strong first century Jewish context to this letter. The Interpreter's Bible calls James "a Christian revision of a Jewish work."[8] By such a comment, I surmise that it is meant that the Greek version of James is a re-working of his original Hebrew teachings. Adam Clarke, a nineteenth century Christian commentator to our book, paralleled some of the contents to *Yalqut Shim'oni*, to the *Mekilta*[9] and to Tractate *Kiddushin* in the Talmud. This is a perceptive insight that he has made for the student of the book of James. The scholar J.D.G. Dunn called James "the most Jewish...document in the New Testament."[10]

It is clear that Ya'akov engages his students and hearers in הלכה מעשית (*halakha ma'asit*); that is, a very practical development and application of the commandments of the Torah. His instructions and teachings are neither ethereal nor philosophical in nature. They are meant to be instructional guides on how to live, focusing on concrete ways to apply Leviticus 19.18b in the day-to-day life of Ya'akov's community: "you will love your fellow man as yourself" (Lev. 19.18b, author's translation).

Thus we understand a crucial part of the background of this book: that Ya'akov is developing *"halakha ma'asit."* That is, first century rabbinic instruction is given on the question of how to understand the Torah commandments. Emphasis is put upon how to keep them in the given community, era and society.[11] This again affirms the connection to the book's definition as a yalqut. This is a logical background, given that Ya'akov was the chief rabbi and spiritual leader of the early Messianic Jewish community in Jerusalem. In the book of James, one can almost hear the echo of Moses teaching these very commandments in the Sinai to the people of Israel. One can hear the faint echo of the exposition of the Musar rabbis of the earlier part of the twentieth century. They were also engaged in teaching and practicing the commandments of the Torah in their age and location, with their given emphasis on the ethical meanings of the commandments.

Chapter Two

PARASHAT KEDOSHIM AND YA'AKOV

Professors Walter Kaiser and Luke Johnson were modern pioneers in research on the book of James. They both wrote about how the book's contents parallel that of Leviticus chapter 19. Indeed, Ya'akov stresses that one should not swear a false oath against another, should not hold back the daily wages of a worker, should not show favoritism in judgment, should not commit slander, should reprove others in a proper manner, and should refrain from holding grudges against others.

We see these very same emphases in the close paralleling of the commandments of Leviticus 19 to the instructions given in Ya'akov's yalqut. The following table, based upon Professor Walter Kaiser's prior, similar table (see bibliography), reflects these connections.

Table 1.1: Parallels Between Leviticus 19 and Th   of James

LEVITICUS 19 verses	BOOK OF J verses
19.12	4.13-15; 5.1.
19.13	5.4
19.15	2.1
19.16	4.11
19.17	5.20
19.18	2.8
19.19; 19.37; 20.8	2.10-12

As we look at these parallels, it appears that the occurring patterns found throughout the book of James are intentional. Here, it may strike a Jewish reader that Ya'akov, or his scribe(s), is doing such patterning purposefully and methodically. One possibility is that Ya'akov was following chapter 19 of the book of Leviticus, verse-by-verse, and commenting on these consecutive verses. Is it possible, then, that he was following consecutive verses in the given parasha text, and commenting upon them? I believe this could have very well been the case. Chapter four in the book of James contains four comments on the content of the parasha text in Leviticus 19. They appear toward the end of his work. This placement gives these comments a physical concentration that is logical if he was commenting upon the parasha. Another two comments on the content of the parasha text are in chapter two, toward the beginning of his yalqut. Although not all of Ya'akov's comments on the parasha are found in a straightforward, methodical and sequential manner in his yalqut, yet the parallels back to the text in Leviticus 19 in each case are clear. Let us examine some of these parallels.

The Masoretic text of Leviticus 19.2 reads:

ולא שבעות בשמי לשקר וחיללת את שם אלוהיך: אני יהוה

(*Velo' tishbe'u veshmi leshaqer vehilalta 'et shem 'Elohayka; 'Ani Adonay*).

"And do not swear an oath in My name, to lie, and so defame your God; I am Adonay" (Lev. 19.2, author's translation). This verse is an instruction to refrain from taking an oath that involves God in any manner, as this belittles God's reputation and name. As Ya'akov either wrote or said:

προ παντων δε, αδελφοι μου, μη ουνυετε μητε τον ουρανον μητε την γην μητε αλλον τινα ορκον ητω δε υμων το ναι ναι και ου ου, ινα μη υπο κρισιν πεσητε.

(*Pro panton de, adelphoi mou, me omnuete mete ton ouranon mete ten gen mete allon tina orkon eto de umon to nai nai kai to ou ou, ina me hupo krisin peseta*).

"Above all, brothers, stop swearing oaths—not 'by heaven', not 'By the earth', and not by any other formula; rather, let your 'Yes' be simply 'Yes' and your 'No' simply 'No', so that you won't fall under condemnation" (5.12, CJB).

In spite of the language difference between the two texts, the Torah-based commandment of Leviticus 19.12 is easily seen as the background to Ya'akov's point in James 5.12. Leviticus 19.16 states:

לֹא תֵלֵךְ רָכִיל בְּעַמֶּיךָ, לֹא תַעֲמֹד עַל דַּם רֵעֶךָ, אֲנִי יהוה

*(Lo telek rakil be'ameyka; lo' ta'amod
'al dam re'eka—'Ani 'Adonai).*

"Do not spread rumors among your people; do not be apathetic to the fate of your fellow; I am Adonai" (Lev. 19.16, author's translation). This is a simple, straightforward instruction forbidding both the spread of rumors, and the presence of apathy in the face of wrongdoing. James 4.11 informs us:

Μη καταλαλειτε αλληλων, αδελφοι. Ο καταλαλον αδελφου η κρινων τον αδελφον αυτου καταλαλει νομου και κρινει νομον ει δε νομον κρινεις ουκ ει ποιητης νομου αλλα κριτης.

(Me *katalaleite, allelon, adelphoi; ho katalalon adelphou he krinon ton adelphon autou kataleli nomon ton krinei nomon ei de nomon krineis, ouk e poetis nomou alla kriteis).*

"Brothers, stop speaking against each other! Whoever speaks against a brother or judges a brother is speaking against *Torah* and judging *Torah*. And if you judge *Torah*, you are not a doer of what *Torah* says, but a judge" (James 4.11, CJB).

Ya'akov begins this piece of instruction with perhaps a direct quote from Leviticus 19.6a (against spreading rumors).

18

He then further embellishes his teaching with an explanation of how spreading rumors is a type of unrighteous judgment (4.11b). Again, the subject of rumors strongly connects our two texts here. In Leviticus 19.17, we read:

לֹא תִשְׂנָא אֶת אָחִיךָ בִּלְבָבֶךָ, הוֹכֵחַ תּוֹכִיחַ
אֶת עֲמִיתֶךָ וְלֹא תִישָׂא עָלָיו חֵטְא

(Lo tisna' et 'ahika bilvavayka; hokeah tokiah 'et
'amitayka velo' tisa' 'alav het).

"Do not hate your brother in your mind; reprove your colleague in honesty, and in doing so you will not sin against him" (Lev. 19.17, author's translation).

This is an encouragement to instruct one's acquaintance when such is wrong about an important issue. This is in opposition to not communicating at all, or spreading rumors about the person, or simply despising the person. Apathy is not an option if one is to fulfill Leviticus 19.17-18, which includes the "royal commandment" (19.18b). Ya'akov draws upon this theme in his yalqut, as he teaches:

Γινωσκετο οτι ο επιστρψας αμαρωλον εκ
πλανης οδου αυτου σωσει ψυχην αυτου εκ θανατου
και καλυψει πληθος αμαρτιων.

(Ginosketo hoti ho epistrepsas amartolon ek
planes odou autou sosei psuken autou ek thanatoo
kai kalupsei plethos amartion).

19

"You should know that whoever turns a   me; from his wandering path will save him from death a   cover many sins" (James 5.20, CJB).

Could Ya'akov's teaching in James 5.20   ve been part of his commentary on Leviticus 19.17-18? Th   ally, there is a development of the theme of "don't hat   brother... reprove your colleague in honesty." Ya'akov   spinoff of what keeping this commandment does for the   he ': it "saves him from death"[1] The rabbinic teaching of "he who saves one life, it is as if he saved a world" is echoed in Ya'akov's statement here.[2] Leviticus 19.18 and James 2.8 bear a strong connection to each other. The Leviticus text states:

לא תיקום ולא תיטור את בני עמך: ואהבת לרעך כמוך ,אני אדוני

(Lo' tiqom velo' titor 'et benay 'ameka; ve'ahavta lere'eka kemoka; 'Ani 'Adonai).

"Do not seek revenge and do not hold a grudge against any of your people; but love your neighbor as your own self; I am Adonai!" (Lev.19.18, author's translation). This verse instructs us to avoid taking vengeance upon any countryman, nor to harbor anger or a grudge against him. Then the instruction is topped off with the general commandment to "love your neighbors as your own self." In many ways, 19.18 became a "beacon" commandment (known as an *av*; see glossary). Yeshua considered it as such in his teaching: "Rabbi, what is the greatest commandment in the Torah? And he said to him, 'You shall love the Lord your God with all your mind, with all your life and with all your resources.' This is the great and beacon commandment. The second is like it, 'You shall love your neighbor as yourself.' These two commandments undergird the entire Torah and the Prophets" (Matthew 22.36-40, translation/paraphrase by author).

The issue of identifying the most comprehensive or important commandment is a subject of rabbinic discussion in ancient times. The following narrative from the Talmud illustrates a like question to the one that Yeshua commented upon in Matthew 22: "On another occasion, it happened that a certain heathen came before Shammai and said to him, 'make me a proselyte, on condition that you teach me the whole Torah while I stand on one foot.' Thereupon he repulsed him with the builder's cubit, which was in his hand. When he went before Hillel, he said to him, 'what is hateful to you, do not to your neighbor: that is the whole Torah, while the rest is the commentary thereof; go and learn it'" (Shabbat 31a, taken from www.comc-and-hear.com/shabbath/shabbath_31.html).

We have a similar discussion in this Talmudic narrative:

Rabbi Simlai taught: 613 commandments were given to Moses, 365 "thou shalt nots," equal to the number of days in the solar year, and 248 "thou shalts," corresponding to the parts of the body... David came and boiled them down to 11, as it is written: Lord, who shall dwell in your sanctuary?... one who lives without blame, who does what is right and in his heart acknowledges the truth; whose tongue is not given to evil, who has never done harm to his fellow or borne reproach for his acts toward his neighbor; for whom a contemptible man is abhorrent, but who honors those who revere

God; who stands by his word, even when it hurts; who has never lent money at an interest or accepted a bribe against the innocent (Psalm 15.1-5). Isaiah came and boiled them down to six, as it is written: One who does what is right, speaks what is true, spurns profit from fraudulent dealings, waves away a bribe instead of grasping at it, stops his ears from listening to infamy, shuts his eyes from looking at evil...(Isaiah 33.15). Micah came and boiled them down to three, as it is written: God has told you, O man, what is good, and what the Lord requires of you; only to do justice, and to love goodness and to walk modestly with your God (Micah 6.8). Isaiah came again and boiled them down into two, as it is written: Thus says the Lord: 'Observe what is right and do what is just' (Isaiah 56.1). Amos came and boiled them down to one, as it is written: For thus says the Lord to the house of Israel: 'Seek Me and live' (Amos 5.4). (Makkot 23b-24a, taken from http//www.avodah.net/assets/Weekly-Torah-Teachings/Bamidbar-Numbers/7-146-Balak-Boil-it-Down-for-Me, 1 August 2011)

Of course, Yeshua did not spontaneously make up this commandment found in Matthew 22. He was teaching about the supreme importance of the instruction given in Leviticus 19.18b. Ya'akov logically found this commandment to be of highest importance, as well.[3] In fact, Ya'akov taught his students to obey this commandment as a priority:

Ει μεντοι νομον τελειτε βασιλικον κατα τεν γραθεν αγαπησεις τον πλησιον σου ως σεαυτον, καλος ποιετε.

(*Ei mentoi nomon teleite Basilikon kata ten graphen agapeseis ton plesion sou os seauton, kalos poiete*).

"If you truly attain the goal of Kingdom *Torah*, in conformity with the passage that says, 'Love your neighbor as yourself,' you are doing well" (James 2.8, CJB).

His appellation of this verse as the "kingly or royal commandment" (*nomon teleite Basilikon*) hints at just how crucial he considered this commandment to be. He too considered it an "av" (see glossary) of the entire body of Torah. Granted, as Yeshua taught on these priorities, he stated that Deuteronomy 6.4 and the belief in the One God, as passed on to us by that verse, was the greatest of all commands. However, he taught that all the commands were connected to *both* loving the One God (cf. Deuteronomy 6.4-9), *and* loving others (Leviticus 19.18b). There is no separation between these two concepts. Ya'akov emphasized that you *cannot* have one without the other. They are an inherent whole. Thus, the connection between Leviticus 19.18 and James 2.8 is clear. In fact, Ya'akov quotes the Leviticus 19.18 text in James 2.8. Buth brings out the background of the idiomatic phrase "royal law" in referring to Leviticus 19.18b. He notes that the phrase חוק חירות (*hoq herut*), "law of liberty" was used by the Qumran community in its writings. Buth quotes the Mishnah, where *herut* ("liberty") is defined as diligence in studying

23

and carrying out the instructions of the Torah: "don't read it 'harut' (engraved) but 'herut' (liberty), because no one is free unless he busies himself in acquisition of the Torah"[4] (Avot 6.2, author's translation).

There is a vital and necessary connection in both ancient and modern Judaism between studying the Torah and living it (i.e. "doing it"). There is no separation of philosophical thought between the concepts of hearing and doing. This is precisely the very strong point made by Ya'akov throughout his entire yalqut! Here is his instruction on this very matter: "Don't deceive yourselves by only hearing what the Word says, but do it! For whoever hears the Word but doesn't do what it says is like someone who looks at his face in a mirror, who looks at himself, goes away and immediately forgets what he looks like. But if a person looks closely into the perfect *Torah*, which gives freedom, and continues, becoming not a forgetful hearer, but a doer of the work it requires, then he will be blessed in what he does" (James 1.22-25, CJB). Gruber translates James 1.25 as "not being a hearer who forgets, but a doer of the work—there is good for this man in what he does."[5]

Ya'akov is repeating what the Torah had taught Jewish students for centuries before him. This is graphically expressed in the Hebrew text of Exodus 24.3 and 24.7 by the phrase נעשה ונשמע (*na'aseh ve'nishmah*), "we will do and we will hear." The Hebrew word order emphasizes the necessity of doing the commandment first, then understanding the rationale and principles behind it, if at all possible. Jewish teachers often expound upon Exodus 24, that the people of Israel *first* responded (and correctly so) that they would carry out the Torah's instructions *as* they were studying it. This is before learning all of its rationales, and its legal and halakhic "ins and outs." As one contemporary commentator wrote: "The statement "we will do, and we will hear," amounts to a commitment to carry out God's commandments even before hearing what the observance of those commandments actually involves. Only someone who is totally willing to shape his entire life around Torah observance would be willing to make such a commitment."The Gemara (circa. late 6th, early 7th century) confirms this understanding, and relays it through the following two *aggadot* (homiletical stories, see glossary). Rabbi Eleazar said: "When the Israelites gave precedence to 'we will do' over 'we will hearken,' a Heavenly Voice went forth and exclaimed to them, 'Who revealed to My children this secret, which is employed by the Ministering Angels, as it is written, Bless the Lord, ye angels of his. Ye mighty in strength, that fulfill his word, that hearken unto the voice of his word': First they fulfill, then they hearken?" (Shabbat 88a, Soncino edition).

The second story is similar: "Rabbi Hama son of R. Hanina said: "What is meant by, 'As the apple tree among the trees of the wood, so is my beloved among the sons'…why were the Israelites compared to an apple tree? To teach you: Just as the fruit of the apple tree precedes its leaves, so did the Israelites give precedence to 'we will do' over 'we will hearken'" (Shabbat 88a, Soncino edition).

Therefore, Ya'akov's emphases in his yalqut, chapter 1.22-25, upholds the well-founded Jewish belief that it is necessary to first carry out the instructions of the Torah, and only then understanding the "whys" behind the instructions themselves. Furthermore, his use of the concepts of the "royal law" (*nomon…basilikon*) and "perfect law" (*nomon teleion*) reflects the very solid Torah base of his teaching. In fact, there is the possibility of translating the phrase "royal law" as "royal Torah" or "royal instruction," depending upon the many ways that the Greek word νομος (*nomos*), "law, Torah or instruction" was used in ancient times. I am suggesting, then, that James 2.8 can be accurately translated as: "If you truly carry out the royal instruction found in the Torah, 'Love your neighbor as yourself,' you do what is good." In this rendition, the King (God) has revealed His instructions in the Written Torah. In the first century, there was no other holy scripture! Ya'akov, of necessity, had to be referring to the Torah in 2.8.

Parashat Kedoshim (see glossary) may have served as the inspiration for Ya'akov's teachings in his yalqut. It is very possible that the Torah's admonition: "Do not swear falsely by my name" (Leviticus 19.12a, NIV) was his springboard for taking up this same subject. Yeshua denounced the making of business pledges with oaths that invoked God's name (cf. Matthew 5.33-37). Ya'akov is teaching against the same practice here. If Leviticus 19.12 was the Torah portion that was read in the Jewish world for that given week, Ya'akov would have had the logical platform by which to address this topic. He taught: "Above all, brothers, stop swearing oaths—not 'By heaven' and not 'By the earth', and not by any other formula; rather let your 'Yes' be simply yes and your 'No' simply no, so that you won't fall under condemnation" (James 5.12, CJB).

Again, Ya'akov taught, "now listen, you who say: 'Today or tomorrow we will go to this or to that city, spend a year there, carry on business and make money.' Why, you do not even know what will happen tomorrow. What is your life? You are a mist that appears for a little while and then vanishes. Instead, you ought to say: 'If it is the Lord's will live, and do this or that'" (James 4.13-15, NIV). In Matthew 5.33-37, Yeshua taught: "Again you have heard that our fathers were told, 'Do not break your oath' and 'Keep your vow to ADONAI.' But I tell you not to swear at all—not 'By heaven', because it is God's throne, nor 'By earth', because it is his footstool; and not 'By Yerushalayim', because it is the city of the Great King. And don't swear by your head, because you can't make a single hair white or black. Just let your 'Yes' be a simple 'Yes' and your 'No' a simple 'No'; anything more than this has its origin in evil" (5.33-37, CJB). These words are repeated nearly verbatim by Ya'akov: "Above all, my brothers, do not swear—not by heaven or by earth or by anything else. Let your 'Yes' be yes, and your 'No', no, or you will be condemned" (James 5.12, NIV). I suspect that this verse may be a *direction quotation* from Yeshua's teaching, as found above in Matthew 5. Furthermore, in Leviticus 19.19, 37 and 20.8, we are taught three times in a short space to keep *the entire Torah* with all its commandments. In the poetry of the biblical narrative, the repetition of something three times in close proximity in the text indicates emphasis![6] Ya'akov's words in James 2.10 could easily have come in connection to this very point: "For whoever keeps the whole law and yet stumbles at just one point is guilty of breaking all of it" (James 2.10, NIV).

With the above connections shown between the relevant texts in Leviticus and the book of James, we can ask another pertinent question: When and how would a Jewish community have taken part in this very type of activity? That is, what may have been the occasion for the type of teaching exposition done by Ya'akov in his yalqut? On the weekly Sabbath, Jewish communities in Ya'akov's time (and today) methodically read and study a portion of scripture, termed the *parasha* (see glossary).[7] I believe that the very parasha portion that Ya'akov comments upon in his yalqut can be identified. It is named *Kedoshim*, and is found in Leviticus 19.1-20.27.[8] The language of Ya'akov's book is considered good literary Greek, even though in part it is quoting spoken words, as if a scribe wrote down the highlights of Ya'akov's parasha lesson/sermon that he heard in person in Hebrew. Such scribe then reiterated them in written Greek. A thorough analysis of the Greek, and how it reflects the spoken original language is the subject of a different study, and could be a key to unfolding what I am suggesting. The cycle of parasha reading in vogue two thousand years ago in Israel was probably a triennial cycle. I am not aware of how similar the parasha portions and their verses were in comparison to today's one year long parasha cycle. In spite of that uncertainty, I am not discouraged from making connections between the book of James and parashat Kedoshim. It is still logical to assume that Leviticus 19.1-20.27, today's parashat Kedoshim, remained intact as a single parasha reading. This entire portion is compact in size and is legal in its contents, making it a single-focused unit.

There is another element in the yalqut that can help us realize its Jewish background. The book bears similarity to the Talmudic tractate *Pirke Avot* ("Chapters of the Fathers," see glossary), in its literary genre and content. The contents of the book of James were taught some one hundred and forty years before the appearance of Pirke Avot in writing. Both the book of James and Pirke Avot are summary teachings of prominent rabbi(s). In the yalqut, we are talking about one rabbi (Ya'akov), while in Pirke Avot, we have the summary teachings of many different rabbis from succeeding generations. Yet, similarities appear in the areas of textual contents and historical background.

Who was the intended audience of the book of Ya'akov? "Ya'akov, a servant of God and of the Master Yeshua the Messiah, to the twelve tribes in the Diaspora" (James 1.1, author's translation). According to this introductory verse, the intended audience, that is, those needing to obtain Ya'akov's yalqut, were Messianic Jewish communities in the Diaspora. In that Ya'akov was the chief rabbi of the Messianic Jewish community in Israel, this makes good historical sense. He had both the authority and the role to serve as the mentor to these Diaspora communities. It is logical to assume that there was need for one standardized set of teachings from Ya'akov to use as an instructional text in these aforementioned communities.

Similarly, even though it was over a century later, the recipients of Pirke Avot were Jewish students both in Israel and in the Diaspora. These young men needed one standardized set of teachings from their rabbis in order to rebuild Judaism after the rampant destruction from two unsuccessful wars against Rome. Thus the Mishnah also consisted of the summary teachings of the most prominent chief rabbis, namely the *nasi* and *av bet din* of their time (see glossary). The urgent need was to get their teachings out to as many Jewish communities as possible. Similarly, the scrolls of Ya'akov's yalqut were also distributed in such a manner as to reach a wanting audience of Messianic Jewish students in the Diaspora.

Chapter Three

WHO WAS YA'AKOV? THE MAN AND HIS INFLUENCE.

I will now endeavor to show how prominent a rabbinic figure Ya'akov was in the ancient Messianic Jewish world. If we understand his importance, we will see why his writings and teachings were a desired item for dispersion into the early Messianic Jewish world.

In Acts 15, a legislative and judicial council of Jerusalem's Messianic Jewish leaders was held in order to decide "halakhic practice". By "halakhic practice", I mean a standard community practice based upon interpretation of the Torah, and decided upon by the community's authoritative body. Such a body of men who decided Torah-based community practices had clearly been lacking in Israel's Messianic Jewish community before 50 AD (which is the author's estimated date of the convening of this council).

A number of non-Jews were becoming followers of Yeshua as the Messiah. This was occurring in various parts of the Roman Empire. Without an authorative Messianic Jewish group of judges and rabbis, *there was no order or agreed upon way* for these new Gentile believers to come to belief in Israel's messiah. Neither was there one standard "halakhic practice" extant as to what the lifestyle of these Gentile believers should consist of after they came to believe in Yeshua the Messiah. In other words, it was not fully agreed upon in the Messianic Jewish world as to what the connection of these new believers to the Jewish world needed to be.

Yet, belief in Yeshua as Israel's Messiah was definitely the entrance portal for these new Gentile believers into the existing Jewish world. Thus, the forming of this council and its tasks were dictated by the community needs at the international level. Therefore, a larger group of Messianic Jewish judges, leaders and rabbis were needed to solve a few issues from brewing chaos, the chief of which was, "what do we do with all these Gentiles coming to belief in our Messiah?" At this council, which I will dub a *sanhedrin* (see glossary), Ya'akov functioned as the chief rabbi and chief justice. We will see him acting in such a role in the historical narrative found in Acts 15: "Some men came down from Judea to Antioch and were teaching the brothers, 'unless you are circumcised, according to the custom taught by Moses, you cannot be saved.' This brought Paul and Barnabas into sharp dispute and debate with them. So, Paul and Barnabas were appointed, along with some other believers, to go up to Jerusalem to see the apostles and elders about this question" (Acts 15.1-2, NIV).

These two verses give us the background for Sha'ul's visit to the Messianic Jewish sanhedrin in Jerusalem. Some unnamed and unspecified Judean believers had come to where

Sha'ul and Barnabas were, and they taught that one had to become legally Jewish before believing in Yeshua as the Messiah. Sha'ul and Barnabas had a different experience, so they argued against this given teaching. Chaos ensued, as no one could invoke a single accepted, valid authority to establish the correct *halakha.*[1] In fact, a Pharisee from Jerusalem (Sha'ul) was disputing against Judeans, *also* from the area of Jerusalem! Who was right? Which of these two sets of Land of Israel-based teachers conveyed the proper approach to the issue? The situation was in disarray. A halakhic decision by an authoritative Messianic Jewish sanhedrin was needed in order to once and for all settle this dispute, and provide direction for proper practice. Yeshua's words given to Shim'on, "whatsoever you loose on earth will be loosed in heaven, and whatsoever you bind on earth will be bound in heaven" denotes the process that this narrative describes. In other words, now the young Messianic Jewish leadership had to make halakhic decisions about their community that would have the backing of Heaven (i.e. "loosed" and "bound" in Heaven).[2] An enforceable, authoritative body of halakha was urgently needed to insure authenticity in community practice as belief in Yeshua as Messiah spread.

We can understand how important and how crucial such an authoritative decision would be. It would impact the lives of the entire believing community worldwide, whether we are speaking of Jewish or Gentile members. Sha'ul and Barnabas were sent by believers in Yeshua back to their home in Israel to learn of the right halakha on this issue:

"So the congregation assigned Sha'ul, Bar-nabba and some of themselves to go and put this question before the emissaries and elders up in Jerusalem" (Acts 15.2b, CJB). They accordingly went off to Jerusalem, to consult with Ya'akov, Shim'on and the inner circle of leaders.

Our text continues: "When they came to Jerusalem, they were welcomed by the Messianic Jewish community and the apostles and elders, to whom they reported everything God had done through them. Then some of the believers who belonged to the party of the Pharisees stood up and said, 'The Gentiles must be circumcised and required to obey the Torah of Moses.' The apostles and elders met to consider this question" (Acts 15.4-6, NIV).

We have a description of the Messianic Jewish sanhedrin that met there: that is, the collection of judges, rabbis and leaders, who decided on the given halakhic issue. Of course, again, the given issue was "must Gentiles first convert in order to believe in Yeshua as the Messiah?" (cf. Acts 15.5). The text continues:

> After much discussion, Shim'on got up and addressed them: Brothers, you know that some time ago God made a choice among you that the Gentiles might hear from my lips the message of the gospel and believe. God, who knows the heart, showed that he accepted them by giving the Holy Spirit to them, just as he did to us. He made no distinction between us and them, for he purified their hearts by faith. Now then, why do you try to test God by putting on the necks of the disciples a yoke that neither we nor our fathers have been able to bear? No! We believe it is through the grace

of our Messiah Yeshua that we are saved, just as they are.' The whole assembly became silent as they listened to Barnabas and Sha'ul telling about the miraculous signs and wonders God had done among the Gentiles through them. When they finished, Ya'akov spoke up: 'Brothers, listen to me'"…(Acts 15.7-13, NIV).

The text records that Shim'on was given the floor to argue his perspective. Why does Luke record Shim'on's words here? Although our text does not state this, in the role of Yeshua's *talmid hakam* ("chief student", see glossary), Shim'on's words and perspective carried special weight.[3] He is given the honor of being quoted by name by Luke, as opposed to just being included in Luke's summary statement: "After much discussion…" This is because Shim'on's role as talmid hakam was to disperse the teachings of his rabbi (Yeshua) after the rabbi's death. Yeshua also gave Shim'on further responsibilities that made him a crucial figure in the disputation (e.g. "feed my sheep"; "upon this rock I will build my movement…"). In addition, Shim'on had the experience of being the first student to share in person about Yeshua's messiahship to a group of interested Gentiles and God fearers.[4]

Sha'ul and Barnabas were then given the floor, as they had firsthand knowledge of the issue at hand. In addition, they were veteran students of Yeshua, with excellent reputations, and with recognized, important roles in the emerging community.

Let us focus on verse 13. When the testimonies had been heard, it was *the role of Ya'akov* to summarize the main points up to then. Then it was his prerogative to offer a final, halakhic

solution on behalf of this entire sa   he   his order of events
in the text makes complete sense   kov is functioning
in the role of chief rabbi and chie   in this sanhedrin.
What we have is the summary stat   the chief rabbi,
which of course would come at the   e deliberations,
and represent the entire sanhedrin in   l outcome. Let
us note Ya'akov's words: "Shim'on h   de   ed to us how
God at first showed his concern by tak ng fro n the Gentiles
a people for himself. It is my judgment, the efore, that we
should not make it difficult for the Gentiles ho are turning to
God. Instead, we should write to them, tell   hem to abstain
from food polluted by idols, from sexual immo ality, from the
meat of strangled animals and from blood. For Moses has been
preached in every city from the earliest time and is read in the
synagogues on every Sabbath" (Acts 15.6-1 , NIV).

With these words, Ya'akov set in moti n the halakha
that has remained for the past 2,000 years.[5] hus, this was
a very powerful, indeed earth-shattering set of decisions. It
opened the doors for non-Jews to believe in the Jewish God
and in Israel's Messiah, as well as gave instruction on how
these new believers were supposed to live as a community.
Ya'akov clearly spoke in the role of community chief rabbi by
his summarizing, and his relaying of the halakhic decision(s).
It is also noteworthy that this sanhedrin appears to have ended
its official deliberations with Ya'akov's words, *because of* his
recognized role.

Some ten or eleven years later, Ya'akov again appears in
the annals of Acts in the same role of chief rabbi/Messianic
Jewish community head in Jerusalem:

The next day Sha'ul and the rest of us went to see Ya'akov, and all the elders were present. Sha'ul greeted them and reported in detail what God had done among the Gentiles through his ministry. When they heard this, they praised God. Then they said to Sha'ul: "You see, brother, how many thousands of Jews have believed, and all of them are zealous for the law. They have been informed that you teach all the Jews who live among the Gentiles to turn away from Moses, telling them not to circumcise their children or live according to our customs. What shall we do? They will certainly hear that you have come, so do what we tell you. There are four men with us who have made a Nazarite vow. Take these men, join in their purification rites and pay their expenses, so that they can have heads shaved. Then everybody will know there is no truth in these reports about you, but that you yourself are living in obedience to the law. As for the Gentile believers, we have written to them our decision that they should abstain from food sacrificed to idols, from blood, from the meat of strangled animals and from sexual immorality." (Acts 21.18-25, NIV).

This text recalls the return of Sha'ul to Jerusalem, in part to share about his travels and experiences with the Jerusalem leaders (i.e. the Messianic Jewish "sanhedrin" and its chief rabbi, Ya'akov). Luke writes that: "...Sha'ul and the rest of us went to see Ya'akov, and all the elders were present" (21.18).

Luke, whom I consider a precise historian, specifically mentions that Sha'ul, and his traveling partners, went "to see *Ya'akov*" (21.18, italics mine). This is precisely because of Ya'akov's role as the chief rabbi of Sha'ul's home community.[6] This happened shortly after Sha'ul's arrival in Jerusalem (the next day) so this specific visit was a high priority. This specific reference of the need to consult with Ya'akov helps us to comprehend Ya'akov's role more precisely.

Furthermore, in Leviticus 19.19, 37 and 20.8, we are taught to keep *the entire Torah* with all its commandments in three places, all within close proximity to each other in the Torah text. This is a known poetic and literary method in Semitic languages to give emphasis to a given point. Ya'akov's words in 2.10 could easily have come in connection to teaching about this very point: "For whoever keeps the whole law and yet stumbles at just one point is guilty of breaking all of it" (James 2.10, NIV).

We also have another section of the book of James that attests to the diligent Torah observance of Ya'akov and his community, and which will give us a better background by which to understand James 5.14-15. This text states, "is any one of you sick? He should call the elders of the church to pray over him and anoint him with oil in the name of the Lord. And the prayer offered in faith will make the sick person well; the Lord will raise him up. If he has sinned, he will be forgiven" (NIV).

Most translations (e.g., NIV) render the Greek phrase in 5.15, 'η ευχη της πιστεως (*he eukay tes pisteos*) as "prayer of faith" or "prayer offered in faith." However, a valid translation could be "*vow* of faith" (italics mine). It is the same word, *euken,* used in Acts 21.23.[7] In Acts 21, Ya'akov and his elders instructed Sha'ul with these words: "There are four men with us who have made *a vow.* Take these men, join in their purification, and pay their expenses, so that they can have their heads shaved. Then everybody will know there is no truth in these reports about you, but that you yourself are living in obedience to the law" (Acts 21.23-24, NIV, italics mine).

Sha'ul is instructed to take part, at the Second Temple, in what I assess to be the ending of a Nazirite vow. We must inquire as to what type of vow (Hebrew *neder*) is intended by Luke when he uses the world *euken.* The parallels between what is written in Acts 21 and Numbers 6 help to clarify the situation. Again, the inclusion of the subject of Nazirite vows as part of this book is not surprising, given the already mentioned item of "oaths" (*shevuot* in Hebrew, based once again on Leviticus 19.12). Rabbi H. Friedman, the well-known editor of the Soncino Edition of the Talmud, has noted "the making of vows would appear to have been a frequent practice in ancient life."[8] A number of Talmudic tractates, including *Nedarim* and *Shevuot,* focus on the subject of vows and oaths, proving to us that the taking up of such was indeed a common practice in first century Israel.

Ya'akov picks up the subject of *shevuot* ("oaths") in chapter four, and a specific type of *neder* ("contractual oath") here in chapter five. As well, he instructs Sha'ul about taking part in a Nazirite vow. In doing this, he confirms to us the popularity of making vows and oaths in his time-period.

The Numbers 6 text on the Nazirite vow reads:

While he has a vow to God, he   s   ate;
he is to grow his hair freely on his s   p.   the
period of his Nazirite vow, no razor i   llc d to
touch his head until the entire period   his ow is
fulfilled...This is the instruction for th Nazirite
on the day that the period of his vow i lfilled.
He is to be brought to the entrance to   Tent of
Meeting, and offer his offering to Gcd: a perfect
year old male lamb, a perfect year old female
lamb, and a perfect ram for a burnt offering and a
peace offering. Then a basket of matza, semolina
flour and cakes baked in oil: matza wafers soaked
in oil, for their grain and drink offerings. And
the priest will offer this before God as his sin
offering, and as his burnt offering...Then at the
entrance to the Tent of Meeting, the Nazirite must
shave the hair from his vow, and put it in the fire
beneath the peace offering. Then the priest must
take the boiled shoulder of the ram, one sheet of
matza, from the basket; and one matza wafer, and
put it into the hands of the Nazirite, after he has
shaved his hair." (6.5b-6a, 14-16, 18-19, author's
translation)

This text matches the details of the instructions given to
Sha'ul in Acts 21.23-24. In both texts, a vow involving shaving
hair, purification rites and expenses appears. This makes the
conclusion for the Nazirite vow evident. My conclusion is that
Ya'akov oversaw the practice of taking up the Nazirite vow
by members of his community. Combined with the support

of the community elders, this was a community statement of faith in God that apparently led to healing. Ya'akov taught that the faithful Messianic Jew, in doing this, would receive healing and forgiveness (see James 5.15). Thus, the action that this group of elders (i.e. Messianic Jewish rabbis/sanhedrin judges) urged Sha'ul to take was overseen by Ya'akov. Sha'ul was encouraged to financially help some Messianic Jewish men end their Nazirite vow.[9] This was done as concrete proof that Sha'ul kept the Torah and its written commandments, as stated in this verse: "…you yourself [Sha'ul] are living in obedience to the law" (Acts 21.24b, NIV). This gives us small insight into the scrupulous Torah observance of Ya'akov. Again, this suggestion given to Sha'ul is very logical and is to be expected from the chief rabbi of the Messianic Jewish community, from the flesh and blood brother of Yeshua himself (cf. Matthew 5.17-19). Acts 21.25, as well, upholds the original decision as communicated by Ya'akov in Acts chapter 15, "however, in regard to the *Goyim* who have come to trust in Yeshua, we all joined in writing them a letter with our decision that they should abstain from what had been sacrificed to idols, from blood, from what is strangled and from fornication" (21.25, CJB).

Once again, this shows that Ya'akov's wisdom and halakhic decision were still upheld for some time after the issuance of the decision.[10] Thus, the Acts 21 text quoted above is consistent with the recognition of Ya'akov as chief rabbi and *Nasi* of this Messianic Jewish community's sanhedrin. As to the role in which Ya'akov continued to function up to the year of his murder in 62AD, Yosef ben Mattityahu the historian noted,[11]

Ananus (High Priest Hananya) was of this disposition; he thought he had now a proper opportunity [to exercise his authority]. Festus (the Roman governor) was now dead, and Albinus (the new governor) was but upon the road; so he (Hananya) assembled the sanhedrin of judges, and brought before them the brother of Yeshua, who was called Messiah, whose name was Ya'akov, and some others, [or, some of his companions]; and when he had formed an accusation against them as breakers of the law, he delivered them to be stoned: but as for those who seemed the most equitable of the citizens, and such as were the most uneasy at the breach of the laws, they disliked what was done; they also sent to the king [Agrippa III], desiring him to send to Ananus that he should act so no more, for that what he had already done was not to be justified; nay, some of them went also to meet Albinus, as he was upon his journey from Alexandria, and informed him that it was not lawful for Ananus to assemble a sanhedrin without his consent. Whereupon Albinus complied with what they said, and wrote in anger to Ananus, and threatened that he would bring him to punishment for what he had done; on which king Agrippa took the high priesthood from him." (Antiquities, Book 20, chapter 9, bracketed information provided by editor of this edition, see bibliography. Information in parentheses mine).

This description of Ya'akov's death highlights his role as chief rabbi of the Messianic Jewish community. Ben Matityahu helps to clarify that Ya'akov was acknowledged as the community's chief leader. Historian Hugh Schonfield wrote: "James the brother of Jesus was elected Nasi, or president of the (Messianic Jewish) supreme council" (The History of Jewish Christianity, H. Schonfield, p.15, no other information given). In spite of this, he was hated by Hananya (Ananus) the Sadducee.[12] The historian Hegesippus (d. 180AD), though not a contemporary to Ya'akov as Ben Mattityahu was, writes about Ya'akov's death, as well. Hegesippus notes that: "James, the Lord's brother, succeeded to the government of the Church, in conjunction with the apostles. He has been universally called the Just, from the days of the Lord down to the present time."[13] I will paraphrase this description into more historically relevant and contextually accurate Jewish terms: "Ya'akov, the brother of Messiah, filled the role of Chief rabbi of the Messianic Jewish community in cooperation with Messiah's inner circle of closest students. He was known worldwide as the *sadiq*,[14] starting in Messiah's lifetime till now."

Hegesippus understood Ya'akov's role to be that of the Chief rabbi of his community, who carried out his tasks in coordination with Yeshua's earlier inner circle of students ("the apostles"). Acts 15 and Acts 21 confirm such cooperation among this group of leaders. I refer the reader to these sections for further study on this matter. Furthermore, Hegesippus relates that Ya'akov was addressed by those who killed him in the following words: "…you [Ya'akov] are just, and show partiality to none."[15] Interestingly enough, part of Ya'akov's

43

letter decries the practice of "sh... partiality" (cf. James 2.1-7). Hegesippus mentions ... s strong reputation for impartiality in the above text... r to possess such a reputation, one would have to se... role of leadership, probably as a judge. Hegesippus p... m...e evidence of Ya'akov's scrupulous Torah observan... ...ng: "Therefore, in consequence of his (Ya'akov's) pre... ...ustice, he was called the Just, and Oblias, which signifi... in... ·k, Defense of the People, and Justice, in accordance w...th... the prophets declare concerning him."[16] The language us... ...y Hegesippus confirms Ya'akov's role as a judge who provi... st decisions in halakhic areas as well as regarding perso... sputes. It is clear that Hegesippus identifies Ya'akov as ... ...ef leader of Israel's early Messianic Jewish community... ...sippus also gives us a view of the influence and popul... hat Ya'akov enjoyed among people both in the city of Jer... m, and in the Jewish world in general.

On one Passover week, when the ... ...al pilgrimage was taking place, Ya'akov was asked to a...dress the crowd of people in the Temple area, because "...for a...l the people, and we also, listen to your persuasion."[17] Additionally, it is of note that the historian Eusebius (d. 339AD.) refers to Ya'akov as "righteous" no less than nine times in his description of Ya'akov's death.

Perhaps Ya'akov taught the Jewish pilgrims (Hebrew, *olim*) from the southern steps of the Temple, which would have been a typical Passover activity (cf. Luke 2.46-47). The chief rabbis of Israel, as well as local and visiting rabbis, taught comers to the Temple during public holidays at various places around the Temple mount.

In sum, by what we can garner from the Newer Testament writings, as well as from the descriptions of Ben Matityahu, Hegesippus and Eusebius, Ya'akov's role was similar to that of the *nasi* in the world of the Great Sanhedrin. Such a role incorporated tasks as a *shofet rashi* ("chief justice"), legislating *halakhic* practice, activity as a teacher of Torah, mentoring students, and having the recognition as the acting head of his community in Jerusalem. We see all of these roles as part of Ya'akov's sphere of influence, as evidenced by the above-mentioned sources. Since he held such a position, it is easy to understand why the book of James was sent around to relevant Diaspora communities for study and guidance purposes. Shanks and Witherington view Ya'akov as the head of his Jewish community, as well: "James was indeed a sage… if one asked members of the first century (Messianic Jewish community) who were their top leaders…they would probably mention James first."[18] The respect shown to Ya'akov in the writings of the Newer Testament is evident by him being mentioned by Yehudah (Jude) in 1.1 of that letter:

Iou/daß ΔIhsouv Cristouv douvloß, aÓdelfo\ß de" ΔIakw¿bou.
(*Ioudas Iesou Kristou doulos, adelphos de Iakobou*).

"Yehudah, servant of Messiah Yeshua, brother of Ya'akov…").

Ya'akov's role in his own community is similar to that of the sages recorded in Pirke Avot (see glossary). From chapter one of Pirke Avot, we see summary teachings of leading rabbis as recorded by their students (and as edited by Rabbi Yehuda ha-Nasi). I will take just a small section from this very chapter to illustrate my point.

> Shmaayah and Avtalyon received from them. Shmaayah would say: Love worship, hate mastery over others, and avoid intimacy with the government. Avtalyon would say: Scholars, be careful with your words. For you may be exiled to a place inhabited by evil elements [who will distort your words to suit their negative purposes]. The students who come after you will then drink of these evil waters and be destroyed, and the Name of Heaven will be desecrated. Hillel and Shammai received from them. Hillel would say: Be of the students of Aaron—a lover of peace, a pursuer of peace, one who loves all creation and draws them close to Torah. He would also say: One who advances his name, destroys his name. One who does not increase, diminishes. One who does not learn is deserving of death. And one who makes personal use of the crown of Torah shall perish. He would also say: If I am not for myself, who is for me? And if I am only for myself, what am I? And if not now, when? Shammai would say: Make your Torah study a permanent fixture of your life. Say little and do much. And receive every man with a pleasant countenance. Rabban Gamliel would say: Find for yourself a teacher; stay away from doubt; and do not accustom yourself to tithe by estimation

(Pirke Avot, chapter one, Mishnas 10-16, accessed from http://www.chabad.org/library/article_cdo/aid/2165/jewish/Chapter-One.htm).

In Mishnas 10-16, three generations of teachers are quoted. In their generation, Shemaya and Avtalyon were respectively *nasi* and *av bet din* of the Great Sanhedrin. Hillel and Shammai stepped into these same roles in their generation, and then Rabban Gamliel was the head of the Sanhedrin in his generation.[19] We can see how these rabbis' main, overall, summary teachings are recorded in Pirke Avot. And in James, Ya'akov's main, overall, summary teachings are recorded—for at least for one portion of the parasha cycle in the given year. This is similar to the sages of Mishnas 10-16 quoted above. Combined, they had many other teachings found in the Talmud, but what we have in these mishnas gives us a general framework by which to understand their emphases. In the case of Shemaya and Avtalyon, they are *not* quoted often in the Talmud. So their summary teachings as presented in Avot are crucial to knowing their emphases as Torah teachers.

Hillel, Shammai (and/or his students) and Rabban Gamliel are oft-quoted and their acts recounted in the Talmud. And their general teachings as found in Pirke Avot give us rich insight into who they were as rabbis. Perhaps Shemaya and Avtalyon's situation best parallels that of Ya'akov—they, too, are seldom quoted in Jewish writings, but still what *is* recorded shows their prominence, humility and the main emphases of their teachings. This lines up best to what the book of James does for us with its portrayal of Ya'akov.

If what I surmise about this yalqut is true, Ya'akov's students memorized/recorded his words during Shabbat lessons(s), and made it an instructional letter, similar to the function of rabbinic *response* (see glossary) for Messianic Jewish communities in the Galut (cf. James 1:1 ff). This yalqut was sent to many such communities because of the vital lessons it teaches (perhaps as commentary to *parashat Kedoshim*). "The Letter of James is intended to prevent the community... from losing its sense of identity," note Shanks and Witherington.[20] That very identity, being a Torah-loving, Messiah following Jewish community, is affirmed by Ya'akov's teachings.[21] Additionally, this author agrees with the insight that "James' letter embodies a concern for faithfully living out the essential teachings of the faith."[22] And it should be stressed that these "essential teachings" were not invented by Ya'akov, or even by Yeshua, but they are found written in the Torah of Moses. Ya'akov presents them in a renewed context for his audience. His students subsequently arranged his words, at least in part of this letter, according to the order of the verses of the parasha.

I do not know if my observations and the conclusions that I draw from them can ever be definitively proven, but I favor them as a framework by which to study the book. If nothing else, my observations and conclusions define and then put his book back into its Jewish world, and into its Jewish context. They also put Ya'akov back into his historical role as his community's chief rabbi. And may I add a personal comment: as the brave leader of an ancient Jewish community, Ya'akov deserves to be returned to his rightful place in history, and back to his people whom he loved. To quote Shanks and

48

Witherington: "The legacy of Luther needs to be left behind when it comes to evaluating (Ya'akov)."[23]

Lastly, if we step back and look what at what occurred through Ya'akov's life, we see that he participated as a Messianic Jewish leader in making *halakha* regarding the entry of Gentiles into the Jewish world via their belief in Yeshua the Messiah. The importance of this step cannot be overestimated in the ensuing history of western civilization, if not that of the world.

Chapter Four

THE TORAH BASED CONCEPTS BEHIND THE GREEK VOCABULARY OF YALQUT YA'AKOV

The book of Ya'akov is written in Koine, that is, the Second Temple era, Greek lingua franca used across the Mediterranean world. Yet Ya'akov's concepts are not a product of the Hellenist world, but of the first century Jewish world. We will examine just a few chosen words and phrases from his book that will illustrate this point. As Gruber noted: "The concepts and definitions remained Hebrew even though the translated appearance of the language was Greek."[1]

In James 1.17, it is written: "the Father of lights" in describing God. The Greek reads "tou patros ton photon," του πατρος των φωτων. This description reflects the Torah's picture of the One God, not any concept from Hellenist pantheism or philosophy. Psalm 118.2 states, "...אלי אדוני ויאר לנו" *('Eli Adonai vaya'er lanu)*, "God is Adonai, and He will shine light for us..." Exodus 14 describes the escape from

Egypt, under the direct guidance (Vho uses light to
protect the tribes of Israel:

> Next, the angel of God, w.) \   :oing ahead
> of the camp of Israel, moved av y   vent behind
> them; and the column of cloud ιc   away from
> in front of them and stood behin. he. It stationed
> itself between the camp of Egyp nd he camp of
> Isra'el — there was cloud and d kness here, but
> light by night there; so that the   lid not come
> near the other all night long (14.1   CJB).

Psalm 78.14 describes this same event i he words:

> (*Vayinahem be'anan yomam vekol halil ah be'or 'esh*)
> ״וינחם בענן י ם וכל הלילה באור אש...״

"and He comforted them in a cloud by day, an ll night long by
the light of fire" (author's translation). Psalm ι describes
God in the words עוטה and כסלמה ("*oteh*" and "*kasalmah*"),
"...wrapped in light as with a robe..." (author's translation).
Light is again a theme connected with God as in Psalm 119:

> (*Ner leragli devareyka ve'or lintivati*)
> ״נר-לרגלי דברך; ואור ילנתיבת״

"Your word is a lamp for my foot, and light on my path"
(Psalm 119.105, author's translation). Isaiah also uses light in
connection with God:

> (*Bet ya'akov leku venelka be'or Adonai*)
> ״בית יעקב לכו ונלכה באור יהוה״

"House of Jacob, let's get up and walk in the light of God" (Isaiah 2.5, author's translation). On a number of other occasions, Isaiah returns to the image of God as a light bearer. For brevity's sake, I will quote just one other example:

(Yotzer 'or uvoray hoshek)

"יוצר אור ובורא חושך"

"I (God) form light, I create darkness," (Isaiah 45.7, author's translation). In speaking about God, the prophet Daniel wrote:

(Unhira imeh shere)

"...ונהירא עמה שרא"

"...and light dwells with him" (Daniel 2.22, author's translation). The use of the image of light to describe what God does for His faithful is taken up by Micah, "אדוני אור לי" *(Adonai 'or li)*, "God is light for me" (Micah 7.8, author's translation).

These few examples suffice to show that the Torah presents God as intimately connected to light: as its Creator, as a user of light for His purposes, and as a giver of light to men (with all of its attached symbolic meanings). When Ya'akov calls God "the Father of lights", he is using a *Torah-based* description.

In the very same verse (1.17), Ya'akov then describes God as the One "παρ ω ουκ ενι παραλλαγε..." *(par ow ouk eni parallage...)* "with whom there is no variation..."

This conception of God's behavior is consistent with Torah thought:

('ani 'Adonay lo' shaniti)

"אני אדוני לא שניתי"

"I am Adonai, I have not changed...." (Malachi 3.6a, author's translation). And:

(Hemah yo'vedu, ve'atah ta'amod)
‏"המה יאבדו ואתה תעמד"‏

"They (the heavens) will vanish, but You will stand!" (Psalm 102.26b-27a, author's translation). The Eternal, unchanging and everlasting nature of God is emphasized in these verses, as well as by Ya'akov in 1.17. This is in stark contrast to the unstable nature of the Greek pantheon of gods, who according to Greek myths and narratives, did not behave in a particularly predictable or consistent manner.

In James 1.18, the phrase λογω αληθειας (*Logou aletheias*); "Word of truth" is used. Colossians 1.5 also uses a near exact phrase, λογω της αληθειας (*Logou tes aletheias*); "Word of truth". In their specific contexts, Sha'ul is referring to the "good news" (cf. Col.1.5); while Ya'akov is using this phrase to refer to a Leviticus 23 Jewish holy day that figuratively describes the role of Jewish believers in Yeshua ("a type of first fruits," James 1.18b). In both instances, the connection to a Torah based background is evident.

Psalm 119 states:

(Sidqateka sedeq le'olam vetorateka 'emet)
‏"צדקתך צדק לעולם ותורתך אמת"‏

"Your righteousness is righteous forever; and your Torah is Truth" (v. 142, author's translation).

54

And again:

(Qarov 'atah 'Adonai vekol mitzvoteyka 'emet)
"קרוב אתה אדוני וכל מצותיך אמת"

"You are close, Adonai, and all Your instructions are truth"
(119.151, author's translation).

It is clearly established in the Torah that God's words, as relayed to mankind through its books, are ultimate truth. That is, the history and moral teachings of the Torah, as well as its depiction of Who God is and how He is to be served, are the foundations for all life. Thus, though both Ya'akov and Sha'ul may be specifically referring to "word of truth" in meaning the news about Yeshua as the Messiah, this phrase uses terminology that is based upon verses of the Torah. And so, God's words as truth are the foundation for the usage of the phrase "Word of truth" in James 1.18. Ya'akov's entire base for using the image of "firstfruits" is found in the meaning of this event, which is described in Leviticus 23. This once again shows us the source of his image.

In James 1.18, the word απαρχην (*aparken*), "firstfruits", is used by Ya'akov or his scribe to describe the nature of Jewish believers in Messiah Yeshua. This word can be connected to the event described in Leviticus 23.10-11:

"דבר אל בני ישראל ואמרת אליהם כי תבאו אל הארץ אשר אני נותן לכם וקצרתם את קצירה והבאתם את עמר ראשית קצירכם אל הכהן: הניף את העמר לפני יאדוני לרצנכמו..."
(Daber 'el beney yisra'el ve'amarta 'elehem ki

tavo'u 'el ha'aretz 'ash   *noten lakem uqsartem*
'et qesirah vaheve ʾ   *mer re'shit qesirkem*
'el hakohen: veheʾ   *ʾmer lifney 'Adonai*
                                    lirsonkem...)

"Speak to the people of Israel and saʸ th ᵃ: 'When you come
to the Land that I'm giving to you, ᵈ yᵒ reap the harvest,
then bring an omer of the first fruits of your harvest to the
priest: and wave the omer before Adon. i for your acceptance;
the priest will wave (it) on the day after the Sabbath" (Lev.
23.10-11, author's translation).

In James 1.18, Ya'akov uses the image of the special
wave offering that took place the day after Passover. Ya'akov
takes his imagery straight from the Torah; the meaning of
this image is found in the calendar based on Leviticus 23.
Though Ya'akov's idea is transmitted to us in Koine, the entire
conceptual framework that is being used is a Torah-based one.
James 1.19 may also be transmitting a Torah concept to us. The
word "akousai", ακουσαι, is describing a state of being where
one is in a position to both hear and then *do* what is written.
"Let every person be quick to listen..." (James 1.19a, CJB). In
context, this refers to being quick to hear the words/teachings/
lessons that are taught by the Torah, the scriptures. Such
would have been the typical material that was listened to by
the people whom Ya'akov addresses, whether in oral teaching
form, or in written form. The Torah was the constant study
text used by both Ya'akov's home community in Jerusalem,
and to the recipients of his yalqut in the Diaspora. Paralleling
this thought, in James1.19a to Exodus 24.7, yields interesting

56

results: "We will do and we will hear" is quite similar to "Let everyone be quick to listen" in their conceptual thrusts.

In that Ya'akov is encouraging his students to be ready to listen and do the instructions given in Torah, he is repeating the same lesson that Moses taught in Exodus 24: "Then he (Moses) took the book of the covenant and read it aloud, so that the people *could hear*; and they *responded*, 'everything that Adonai has spoken, we will do and obey'" (24.7, CJB). Ya'akov is instructing his students to be in the same frame of mind that Moses' respondents were in (when they collectively uttered their response as recorded in Exodus 24.7). "Akousai" parallels the action of "shema" in Hebrew (cf. Deut. 6.4), and is *a state of being where hearing and doing God's instructions is a foremost characteristic* of the national purpose (italics mine).

In James 1.22, Ya'akov issues an instruction that is a common theme in rabbinic literature: "Do not merely listen to the word, and so deceive yourselves. Do what it says (1.22, CJB). This same concept is found in Tractate Pirke Avot, where it is written: "Study (of the holy texts) is not the main (activity), but the doing (of it)." (Avot 1.17, author's translation). This is a highlighted teaching of Shim'on ben Gamliel, who in all likelihood was a Jerusalem–based, contemporary Pharisaic authority to Ya'akov. Both of these honored teachers stressed that study is complemented by doing what is written, and without the latter, the former is incomplete. This is a major theme in common between the Pharisees, as represented in Shimon's teaching, and the Messianic Jewish community of early Jerusalem, as represented in Ya'akov's words. This entire idea is based in the Torah, and had not been influenced by the outlying Hellenistic world. It is expressed in Koine in

57

Ya'akov's yalqut; yet, its heart, soul and meaning are a basic foundation of Jewish belief throughout history.

James 1.27 also begs for seeing a Torah–based foundation: "Religion that is pure and undefiled before God and the Father is this: to visit orphans and widows in their tribulations; keep one's self ritually pure from the world" (1.27, author's paraphrase).

Where did first century Jews learn about the merits of spending time with widows and orphans? Ya'akov did not originally conceive of this idea.

"You will not cause distress to any widow or orphan" (Exodus 22.22, author's translation). And again, it is written: "Be joyful at your Feast—you, your sons and daughters, your menservants and maidservants, and the Levites, the aliens, the fatherless and the widows who live in your towns" (Deut. 16.14, NIV). From the verse in Deuteronomy, we learn that it was the responsibility of the entire people to help care for the needs of orphans and widows in their locales. Therefore, the instruction of Ya'akov in James 1.27 is solidly anchored in verses of the Torah. The Koine text of Yalqut Ya'akov cannot obscure this fact.

In chapter two of Yalqut, Ya'akov opens with what sounds like an Eastern Orthodox, high Church title: κυριου ημων Ἰησου Χριστου *(kuriou emon Iesou Kristou)*, "Our glorious Lord Jesus Christ," James 2.1, NIV). But it is not. It *is* an ancient Jewish method, expressed here in Koine, of saying something similar to "admor" in more modern Hebrew parlance. אדמור *(admor)*, is Hebrew for "our lord, our teacher and our rabbi." Other Hebrew terms exist by which to honor a rabbi or teacher. One is שליט"א *(shelita)*, meaning, "May he have a long life full of good days, amen." Another is הקדוש

רבנו (*rabbenu hakadosh*), "our holy rabbi". It was then, and is today, a Jewish custom to give an appellation of honor, or to recite a blessing, when in the presence of a scholar, rabbi or dignitary. It is probable that Ya'akov used such a known term to his Diaspora students in verse one. They would have implicitly understood that he was honoring their Messiah.

James 2.1-17 expresses the mitzvah of משוא פנים (*mas'o panim*), that is, the prohibition of showing favoritism in judgment or action. This is solidly founded upon the Torah's teaching on this subject, found in a number of places. This includes Parashat Kedoshim, where it is written: "Do not pervert justice; do not show partiality to the poor or favoritism to the great, but judge your neighbor fairly," Lev.19.15, NIV). This instruction is repeated in Deuteronomy 1.17, 10.17 and 16.19. Ya'akov points out that showing favoritism is a transgression of the Torah, even though he does not specifically mention which verses are transgressed: "But if you show favoritism, your actions constitute sin, since you are convicted under the Torah as transgressors" (James 2.9, CJB). In James 2.9, Ya'akov uses the word αμαρτιαν (*amartian*), "sin", to describe what he means.

It is in the above–mentioned verses of the Torah where we learn not to show favoritism in the matters of which Ya'akov speaks. Showing favoritism is a transgression of God's instructions on how to live. Showing favoritism in wider first century society was a given political trait in the Roman Empire. Certainly both Roman (and other) histories from that period were fraught with the showing of political favoritisms. The Herodian dynasty histories reek of the same favoritisms. The Torah stands out in the world of the first century Roman

Empire with its teaching again ie very methods often used
to promote one's political and s ial standing in that world.
The gaining and granting of vo was often based not upon
merit, but upon other non–rig us factors. Thus, once again,
the Torah undergirds what Ya'a ov teaches in James 2.1-17.

In James 2.21-24, we ha idrashic point made by
Ya'akov, which he bases upon   in the book of Genesis
(chapter 22): "Wasn't *Avraham* declared righteous
because of actions when he offereu up is son Yitz'chak on
the altar? You see that his faith worked ith his actions; by
the actions the faith was made complete; and the passage of
the *Tanakh* was fulfilled which says, 'Avraham had faith in
God, and it was credited to his account as righteousness.' He
was even called God's friend. You see that a person is declared
righteous because of actions and not because of faith alone"
(CJB). Enough said. Clearly, the foundation and source of his
teaching point are found in the Torah.

James chapter three, verse 12, notes that: "My brothers, can
a fig tree bear olives, or a grapevine bear figs? Neither can a salt
spring produce fresh water…" In his teaching on the proper use
of our words, Ya'akov references the botany and water supply
of the land of Israel. Now, to be technically correct, I suppose
it is possible that Ya'akov could have been talking about a
landscape in Greece, Italy, Turkey or the Levant, which would
also match his same description. However, figs, olives and
grapes all were part of Israel's natural fruitfulness: "…a land
of wheat and barley; and grapevines, figs and pomegranates; a
land of olives, oil and honey" (Deut. 8.8, author's translation).
The three items mentioned by Ya'akov are all included in this
list of Israel's native food supply.

Chapter three continues with verse 13, where Ya'akov's hearers are encouraged to be "wise"; to exhibit "understanding" via "deeds" performed in "humility" that spring forth from "wisdom": "Who is wise and understanding among you? Let him show it by his good life, by deeds done in the humility that comes from wisdom" (3.13, NIV, with one adjustment by the author). The theme of "wisdom" is developed in both Jewish and Hellenist philosophical writings. So the relevant question is which type of wisdom is being talked about here: that which adheres to a Jewish definition, or to a more Hellenized one? The answer to this question is clear.

An entire book could be written on the Jewish concept of σοθος (*sophos*), that is "wisdom" and "wise persons", given by the term we encounter in James 3.13. The books of Proverbs, Ben Sira, and Qohelet (Ecclesiastes), as well as that "wisdom" that was displayed by biblical figures, displays the Jewish concept of "wisdom." The Hellenist concept of "wisdom" differs in large part from the biblical concept of "wisdom" (as expressed by the Hebrew word חכמה [*hokmah*]).[2] It is not in the scope of this essay to compare the Torah concept of "wisdom" with first century Hellenist thought on this subject. Suffice it to say, the contents defining the word "wisdom", and the makeup of the "wise" person differ substantially between biblical and Hellenist thought. This disparity may not necessarily have affected the influence of Hellenism on ancient Judaism, where scholars have long debated how deeply Hellenist thought colored Jewish life during the Second Temple era.

When Ya'akov instructs his students to be "wise" and exhibit "understanding", he surely does so with the framework of Proverbs 9.10 in mind:

"תחילת חכמה יראת אדוני ודעת קדשים בינה"
(*Tehillat hokmah yir'at 'Adonai veda'at qedoshim binah*)

"The beginning of *wisdom* is the fear of Adonai; and knowledge about holy things is *understanding*" (author's translation and italics).

This one verse incorporates both elements of James 3.13—"wisdom" and "understanding"—tying both into their foundation of fearing God. Thus, taking חכמה (*hokmah*) as the cognate to "wise" (Greek, sophos) and "wisdom" (sophias), and taking בינה (*binah*) as the cognate to "epistemon", we should understand Ya'akov's statement as firmly based in the thought of Proverbs 9.10. We could ask the question as to whether Ya'akov could have been thinking of Proverbs 9.10 or Proverbs 2.1-2 as he taught James 3.17? These two verses from Proverbs are remarkably similar to the points he is making. They are both found in the same book, and relevant to his point. In Proverbs 2.1-2, wisdom leads to understanding:

"בני אם תקח אמרי ומצוותי תצפן אתך להקשיב
לחכמה אזנך תטה לבך לתבונה"

(*Beni, 'im tiqah 'amaray umitzvotay tispon 'itak lehaqshiv lahokmah 'ozneyka tateh libeka latvunah*)

"My son, if you take my words and my instructions, then internalize them, and listen to the wisdom with your ears, turning your mind to understanding..." (2.1-2, author's translation).

In Proverbs 2.2, the Hebrew uses a poetic parallelism— חכמה, "hokmah" and תבונה "tevunah" are paired together in the rhythm, with the effect being to lump wisdom and understanding as two parts of the correctly lived life, that is, a life lived by a "fearer of G-d".[3] We cannot definitively answer the question posed above concerning a connection between Proverbs 2 and 9 with James 3.17. Yet, it is logical to assume that the path to attaining wisdom and understanding as conceived of by Ya'akov was that of the author of the Psalms, and not that of Platonism, nor that of the Stoics or Cynics.

In James 4.5, Ya'akov brings up the term η γρθη (*he graphe*)"; "the scriptures". The Hellenist philosophical schools and mystery cults did not have a single body of scripture by which to express, learn and teach their belief systems. There was no parallel to the books of the Torah. In Judaism, of course, it was these very books of the Torah that constituted "the scriptures". By context and logic, the Torah is what Ya'akov is referring to in this verse as "the scriptures". In fact, he then quotes from the Bible in his ensuing words (cf. James 4.5b), proving this assertion.

James 4.6 and 4.10 extol the character trait of being humble. These are the Koine: words ταπεινοις (*tapenois*) and ταπεινωθητε (*tapenothete*), respectively. In verse 4.6, Ya'akov quotes from Proverbs 3.34, which teaches: "To scorners, He will show scorn; but to the humble, He will give favor" (author's translation). If Ya'akov's scribe translated from the Hebrew text, the word "'anavim", ענווים or "'oni'im", עונים, would have been the word translated as "tapenois". If the scribe simply quoted from the Septuagint, the same word "tapenois" is used in that version for "'anavim" or "'oni'im". To any first

63

century Jewish community, being humble was a p   trait,
and an open door to God's blessings. This idea ha   ise *in*
the Torah, where, as an example, it is written in Nu   s 12.3:

(*veha'ish moshe 'anav me'od miko   adam*)
"...האדם מכל מאד ונע ה   "והאי

" And the man Moshe was more humble th   yone"
(Numbers 12.3, author's translation).

Moses was known as the leader, general,   rator,
prophet of God, teacher and visionary par excellei   hus,
emulating his trait of humbleness was certainly   ious
pursuit. Yeshua's own words were known by all of   ov's
students: πραος ειμι και ταπεινος, (*praos eimi kai t   inos*);
"I am meek, and humble in mind" (Matthew 11.29,   thor's
translation). The book of Matthew in 11.29 uses the same
term for "humbleness/meekness" as Ya'akov uses in James
4.6—"tapeinos".

Thus, Ya'akov's exhortation to his students to be humble
is one that is founded in Torah and in the teachings of his Holy
Rabbi Yeshua. Whether this character trait was also valued in
Hellenist culture is not within the scope of this essay to assess,
nor would such existence negate any part of my above points.

James 4.7 relays a belief in an evil personage needing to
be resisted, which permeates the world in an attempt to oppose
believers in Messiah. It is termed "diabolos" ("diabolo" in
our given text). Such an entity has its historical base in the
Prophets (cf. Isaiah 14.12ff). Verse 4.9 is an exhortation that
has parallels in the Torah: "Wail, mourn, sob! Let your laughter
be turned into mourning and your joy into gloom!" (James 4.9,

CJB). Πενθησατε (*penthesate*) is the word used in this verse for wailing or mourning.

First, the call to "wail (and) mourn" signifies an important part of the process of repentance and turning back to God. In the following scriptures, that is the significance of wailing and mourning: Isaiah 22.9-12, Isaiah 61.2-3 and Zechariah 12.10-12. Let us examine Isaiah 22:"You saw how many breaches there were in the City of David, you collected water from the lower pool, you surveyed the houses in Yerushalayim, tearing some down to fortify the wall. You also built a reservoir between the two walls for the water from the Old Pool; but you didn't look to Him who made these things; you had no respect for Him who fashioned them long ago. That day Adonai, the God of the Heavenly Armies, called on you to *weep and mourn*, to shave your heads and wear sackcloth…" (22.9-12, CJB, with one change by the author; italics are by the author). Isaiah describes the foreseen defensive actions of Jerusalem during the Assyrian ruler Senchariv's campaign against Judah. The Hebrew words used for "weep and mourn" are בכי (*beki*), and מספד (*misped*). They are given to us in the above text as a poetic couplet, as is often done in Hebrew poetry in order to emphasize a point. The citizens of Jerusalem had taken action to survive the siege and attack; however, they did not turn back toward God (expressed in the phrase, "to look to Him," and in the idiom: "to see Him". Our text reads:

"ולא הבטתם אל עשיה ויצרה מרחוק לא ראיתם"
(*Velo hibatetem 'el 'oseha veyosrah merahoq lo're'item*)

"But you didn't look to its Maker; and its Fashioner; from afar, you didn't notice!" (Isaiah 22.11, author's translation). It is highly possible that Ya'akov is following the thought process already established by the Torah, such as in the verses above from Isaiah. Ya'akov is encouraging his students to turn back to God in an area of life where they have strayed. Isaiah speaks to his society in a similar vein. The gist of the weeping and mourning, whatever it specifically consists of, is to help the individual (and the larger group) to turn back to God. Similarly, Yeshua taught: "Those who πενθουντες (*penthountes*); "mourn" have a reason to bend their knee in thanksgiving, for they will be comforted" (Matthew 5.4, author's translation). My framework for Matthew 5 leads me to believe that Yeshua was calling for a return to God via one's attitude in verse 5.4. Thus, his meaning for "mourning" would parallel that of Ya'akov's usage for "weeping and mourning". To weep and mourn was to get into the state of turning back to God; then accepting and practicing His ways. Isaiah purposes the same definition for "mourn" in Isaiah 61, as does Zechariah in his chapter 12. The mourning, the weeping, are outward signs of leaving the old attitude, and proofs of a preliminary step towards a full turning to God. Thus, Ya'akov's phrase "wail, mourn, sob" and use of "mourning" and "gloom" in James 4.9 belie a rich background in the Torah. These are all signs of the repentance process in then Jewish society (and some still remain as signs of such in the contemporary Jewish world).

James 4.11 contains an issue that is developed in the Torah as well as in rabbinic literature. "Brothers, stop speaking against each other! Whoever speaks against a brother or judges a brother is speaking against Torah and judging Torah. And if you judge Torah, you are not a doer of what Torah says, but a judge" (CJB).

Ya'akov picks up on the subject of proper and improper speech, touching on categories of such that may include "lashon hara, hotse'et shem ra, dibah" and "sarah" (see glossary for approximate definitions). These four Hebrew terms became legal categories in Jewish jurisprudence of the improper use of speech. Ya'akov's foundation for James 4.11 may include a good number of verses from the Torah, including from our much aforementioned parashat Kedoshim (e.g. Leviticus 19.11-12—against denying the truth, and lying; Leviticus 19.16—against spreading rumors; this verse is considered by classical Jewish sources as teaching against *lashon hara* [see glossary]; Leviticus 19.17-18—proper use of speech to settle a difference). As well, other Torah sources exist for Ya'akov's statement (one such being Deut. 13.15, an instruction that is against the spread of rumors). The Torah.org website lists a number of Torah verses that prohibit wrongful speech, including the following: Exodus 23.1-2, Leviticus 25.17, Deuteronomy 19.15, 24.8-9 and Numbers 17.5. Psalm 34.12-13 also bears relevance to our topic. The website mentioned above lists a more comprehensive list, and I refer the reader to it.

In James 4.11, Ya'akov stresses that it is a person's duty to perform the instructions given to us in the Torah. He points out that verbally abusing another person makes us stand outside the framework of the Torah. Ya'akov notes that committing a verbal abuse assumes that we function in the role of judges of what is right and wrong in the matter of permitted and forbidden speech (when the Torah was meant to be our source for understanding proper speech). Instead of doing what is written, the verbal abuser unsuccessfully attempts to take on the role of God, trying to be the Judge and Authority on what is right and proper: "There is but one Giver of Torah; He is also the Judge, with the power to deliver and to destroy. Who do you think you are, judging your fellow human being?" (James 4.12, CJB).

It is my opinion that Ya'akov drew upon the Torah's teaching in order to express himself in James 4.11 (and 12), and perhaps his exhortation here is part of his parasha commentary for parashat Kedoshim.

James 5.3 brings us to a term that betrays its Torah-centered meaning. The phrase εν εσκαταις ημεραις (*en eschatais hemerais*), is used. This refers to the period known as the "last days", and it has a Hebrew source: אחרית הימים (*aharit hayamim*); literally meaning "end of the days", and possibly ביום ההוא (*beyom hahu*); "on that day". These are two Torah phrases that teach about this same time period. The phrase used in yalqut Ya'akov in Koine, betrays a clear Torah and Jewish based concept of the human historical time line: "... your gold and silver have corroded, and their corrosion will be evidence against you and will eat up your flesh like fire! This is the "acharit-hayamim", and you have been storing up wealth!" (James 5.3, CJB).

As Ya'akov refers to the final period in human history, he knows that accrued wealth will disappear. The priority system of the persons he is instructing is incorrect; this period (the "aharit hayamim") is presented by Ya'akov as a period needing other priorities from his Messianic Jewish students. I refer the reader to James 5.4-5 for further development of Ya'akov's point and challenge to his audience. I will say that once again, he stressed keeping the instructions of the Torah, with paying a worker his daily wage (cf. Deut. 24.14-15), emerging as one of them.

I love the illustration used by Ya'akov in James 5.7. It attests to Ya'akov's connection to the Land of Israel, his homeland: "So, brothers, be patient until the Lord returns. See how the farmer waits for the precious "fruit of the earth" — he is patient over it until it receives the fall and spring rains" (5.7, CJB). Certainly there are seasonal rains over lands of the Mediterranean basin. Yet, the fall and spring rains referred to by Ya'akov are crucial to life in Israel, and made possible the entire yearly crop production of the Land in ancient times. Ya'akov here describes for us the agricultural angst of the Israeli farmer during this period, until the crops were growing, paralleling the waiting for that growth to appear with waiting for Messiah's return. The unique period known as the counting of the Omer was the yearly period during which farmers would inspect their crops for signs of growth (this occurred during the period between Passover and Shavuot; cf. Leviticus 23.15-16). Perhaps Ya'akov is referring to the image of watching one's fields during the period of the counting of the Omer, which would constitute another use of biblical imagery.

James 5.11 states: "Look, we regard those who persevered as blessed. You have heard of the perseverance of Iyov, and you know what the purpose of Adonai was, that Adonai is very compassionate and merciful" (CJB). We are given two evidences in this verse of the rich Torah background of yalqut Ya'akov. First, Iyov (Job) is a book of the Torah, with the fact that it is quoted here serving as a clear proof of the source of Ya'akov's encouragement: the story of Job, i.e., part of Torah. Secondly, the description of Adonai as "very compassionate and merciful" may be a direct quote from Exodus 34: "And he passed in front of Moses, proclaiming, 'Adonai, Adonai, the compassionate and gracious God, slow to anger, abounding in love and faithfulness, maintaining love to thousands, and forgiving wickedness, rebellion and sin'" (34.6-7a, NIV).

Ya'akov bases his description of God's character in James 5.11 on the truth already established in Exodus 34, that Adonai is a merciful God.

James 5.13 gives reference to another piece of the Torah, namely, the Psalms.

"Is someone among you in trouble? He should pray. Is someone feeling good? He should sing songs of praise" (5.13). In our text, the Koine word ψαλλετω (*psaleto*) "psalms" is used. Very possibly Ya'akov was instructing them to sing from the book of Psalms. This would be no big surprise; the Jewish pilgrims to the Temple already did that—and the daily worship in the Temple had a "psalm of the day" sung by the Levitical choir as part of Temple worship ritual. Psalms 113-118 are termed in Hebrew the הלל (*hallel*), i.e. "the praise". It was a known worship text in those times. It continues to be included today in the Jewish siddur (prayer and worship book), as well as in the Haggadah (the Passover meal guide; see glossary). Certainly, in late Second Temple period times, the Psalms were in large part committed to memory, making the logic of my assumption quite possible.

James 5.16 includes Ya'akov's instruction to his students about receiving prayer from a δικαιου (*dikaiou*), a "righteous person." He taught, "The prayer of a righteous person is powerful and effective"(5.16, CJB). In the following two verses, Ya'akov offers an example of a righteous man's prayer being "powerful and effective": "Eliyahu was only a human being like us; yet he prayed fervently that it might not rain, and no rain fell on the Land for three years and six months. Then he prayed again, and heaven gave rain, and the Land produced its crops" (5.17-18, CJB).

Elijah (Eliyahu in Hebrew) is thought of in Jewish tradition as being the epitome of the holy and righteous prophets of Israel. Ya'akov chooses him to illustrate how the influence of a "dikaiou" works. Elijah's prayers were heard by God on high, as Ya'akov notes. Yet, Ya'akov stresses that Elijah was a human being, just like Ya'akov's own students were: "Eliyahu was only a human being like us... (James 5.17a)." Verse 5.16 seems to indicate that the empowering factor in Elijah's prayer was his righteousness. In Judaism, until today, prayer offered by a well known, God fearing rabbi is much desired. This is particularly true in Hasidic communities, where the "tsaddik" (a Hasidic movement's lead or chief rabbi/s) is thought of as a holy man. Consequently, his prayers are considered especially effective. Today and throughout history, the graves of famous Hasidic rabbis are visited by Hasidic students, in hopes that the merit of the given "tsaddik" will benefit the visitor. Pilgrims leave written notes (called a "kvitel" in Yiddish) at these gravesites, in order to ask God's favor. This is similar to the custom of leaving notes in the cracks and crevices of the large stones of the Western Wall in the Jewish Quarter of Jerusalem.

Part of the reason that Yeshua found himself surrounded by crowds and "grabbed" by them on occasion had to do with the fact that he was perceived as a holy and righteous rabbi, and thus his prayers and even physical contact with him would have a beneficial effect, and bring on the favor of God:

> As he went, the crowds on every side virtually choking him, a woman who had had a hemorrhage for twelve years, and could not be healed by anyone, came up behind him and touched the *tzitzit* (ritual fringes) on his robe; instantly her hemorrhage stopped. Yeshua asked, "Who touched me?" When they all denied doing it, Kefa said, "Rabbi! The crowds are hemming you in and jostling you!" But Yeshua said, "Someone did touch me, because I felt power go out of me." Seeing she could not escape notice, the woman, quaking with fear, threw herself down before him and confessed in front of everyone why she had touched him and how she had been instantly healed. He said to her, "My daughter, your trust has saved you; go in peace. (Luke 8.42-48, CJB, parenthesis and comment mine)

Crowds of people hovered around this holy person, pressing in on him. No doubt, this was due to wanting to be close to him, so that his presence, his virtue and his very words would affect them. The above verses show Yeshua to be full of a powerful, holy presence (termed "kedusha" in Hebrew) that healed when it came into contact with disease and defilement. I refer the reader to the relevant essay "Beginning with the End" in *Israel's Messiah and the People of God* by Mark Kinzer (see bibliography), which further explains this particular phenomenon.

Perhaps the following narrative story (termed an "aggadah") as found in the Talmud sheds light on the idea of why a person's prayers are heard:

Another incident occurred concerning Rabbi Hanina ben Dosa, who went to study Torah with Rabbi Yohanan ben Zakkai; his (Yohanan's) son became ill. Rabbi Yohanan ben Zakkai said to him, "Hanina, my son, ask God to have mercy so that he (Yohanan's son) will live; he (Hanina) put his head between his legs, and asked God to have mercy, and so he (Yohanan's son) did live. Rabbi Yohanan ben Zakkai responded: "If I would have stuck my head between my legs all day long, this would not have helped him (his son)." His wife told him: "This is because Hanina is greater than you!" He answered her: "No, it's because he (Hanina) is like a servant before the King, and I am like a government official before the King. (Berakhot 34b, author's translation)

In the aggadah, Rabbi Hanina (d. approx. mid-first century AD) was known for working wonders. Here he prays for the son of the acting chief rabbi, who was also Israel's leading scholar, Rabbi Yohanan. After the prayer of Hanina, God does the healing miracle and heals Rabbi Yohanan's son. The analysis of Rabbi Yohanan, that Hanina is close to God and always stands before God's presence, is very enlightening. *This is given as the reason* that God answered the strange looking prayer (offered by Hanina with his head between his legs). Yohanan did not believe that he held this same status in the Heavenly realms. Instead, he saw himself as an official who is summoned for consultation, and then dismissed from the

73

King's presence in order to perform his role. But the servant (i.e. Hanina) is always with the King. This aggadah shows us that in Ya'akov's time period, there was mainstream belief that the actions of a righteous man was known to be close to God were helpful and influential.

My point is that Ya'akov's emphases in vv.16-17 are well founded in Torah thought, and in his contemporary Jewish tradition and practice. Both Rabban Yohanan and Rabbi Ya'akov are teaching that the prayers of a person who is thought to be close to God are considered valuable to receive. The merit, or righteousness of the "tsaddik" or "dikaios" influences God to hear and act upon the given prayers. Ya'akov encourages his students to pray for each other for healing (which instruction implies that his students are considered righteous before God). Because Ya'akov is the chief rabbi of this authoritative community, his assurances to this end would be very convincing.

James 5.14-15 has a rich Torah-centered background. The text states: "Is anyone sick among you? Let him pray. Is anyone cheerful? Let him sing psalms. Is anyone among you sick? Let him call to the elders of the congregation, and let them pray for him, having anointed him with oil in the name of the Messiah, and the 'euche' of faith will save the ill, and the Messiah will raise him up; if he has committed sin, it will be forgiven him" (author's translation). The word ευχη (euche) is of interest to us in understanding this passage. The NEV version translators inform us that: "The noun euche can also mean a vow, and of its three uses, twice it is used to mean vow (Acts 18:18; 21:23) and once to mean prayer (James 5:15).[4] The understanding of "euche" in the above passage as "prayer" is the interpretation of

74

the NEV translators. However, if "euche" can to be understood to mean the taking of a Nazirite vow, then Ya'akov's statement unveils a solidly based Torah idea. The question is what does "euche" indicate in this passage.

The historian Ben Mattityahu informs us that Nazirite vows were known to be taken by sick persons, in hopes of being healed: "It is usual with those that had been afflicted either with a distemper, or with any other distress, to make vows; and for thirty days before they are to offer their sacrifices, to abstain from wine, and to shave the hair of their heads"[5].

Although he is commenting on the "Esther-like" attempt of Bernice to save people's lives from Florus and the Roman occupiers in this example, the fact that illness was a reason to take this vow seems to be confirmed by him. Although illness is not given in the Torah as a specific reason to take a Nazirite vow (cf. Numbers 6), the fact that Ben Mattityahu mentions sacrifices, along with abstention from wine and shaving as parts of this vow, make it clear that he refers to the Nazirite vow.

Even the possibility of understanding "euche" as a vow in James 5.14-15 opens up the chance that this is what he was instructing his students in Jerusalem to do. Acts 21 would seem to provide an example of this type of vow. Sha'ul and his entourage had just arrived in Jerusalem, and were visiting Ya'akov. Luke records what Ya'akov (and/or the elders who served with Ya'akov) instructed Sha'ul to do: "So, do what we tell you. We have four men who are under a vow. Take them with you, be purified with them, and pay the expenses connected with having their heads shaved. Then everyone will know that there is nothing to these rumors, which they have heard about you; but that, on the contrary, you yourself stay in line and keep the *Torah*. The next day Sha'ul took the men, purified himself along with them and entered the Temple to give notice of when the period of purification would be finished and the offering would have to be made for each of them" (Acts 21.23-24,26, CJB).

It of note, of course, that Ya'akov presided over this very community, and thus there would be consistency between his teaching in the yalqut in verses 5.14-15 and in his instructions to Sha'ul, as recorded by Luke. It is clear that the four Messianic Jewish men who are being referenced by Luke were ending their Nazarite vow. The Acts 21 text brings out the need of the four men to shave their hair, which matches the same need relayed by Numbers 6: "Then at the entrance to the Tent of Meeting, the Nazirite must shave off the hair that he dedicated. He is to take the hair and put it in the fire that is under the sacrifice of the fellowship offering. After the Nazirite has shaved off the hair of his dedication, the priest is to place in his hands a boiled shoulder of the ram, and a cake and a wafer from the basket, both made without yeast" (Numbers 6.18-19). An offering, προσφορα (*prosphora*) is mentioned in the Acts 21 text, paralleling the Numbers 6 offerings that are required, namely the קרבן (*korban*) of Numbers 6.14. "Korban" is used as the general word for "offering", which is then specified in the text. Included are the sin offering, that is, the חטאת (*hattat*—see Numbers 6.14), the whole burnt offering (that is, the עולה, *olah* of Numbers 6.14), and the peace offerings (that is, the שלמים, *shlemim*). Numbers 6.15 continues on with the grain offering (the מנחה, *minha*) and the drink offering (נסך, *nesek*). The vow of the Nazirite was expensive to break, and so the request by Ya'akov and his elders to Sha'ul, to participate

76

in paying for these four men to break their Nazirite vows, is quite understandable. The ability to pay for Nazirite vows to be ended was a rabbinic injunction to the written Torah (termed a תקנה, *takkanah*, see glossary).

By those few but convincing connections, the Nazirite vow comes into play in the Acts text. This is consistent with the use of the Nazirite vow in the early Messianic Jewish community, as presided over by Ya'akov. "Hegesippus...seem(s) to confirm that James was a Nazirite or took on Naziritic vows from time to time."[6]

With even a possibility of "euche" referring to a Nazirite vow, once again the Torah background of Ya'akov's teaching emerges.

James 5.17 refers to the narrative in 1 Kings 18.41-46: "Elijah was a man just like us. He prayed earnestly that it would not rain, and it did not rain on the land for three and a half years. Again he prayed, and the heavens gave rain, and the earth produced its crops" (James 5.17-18, NIV). The text in 1 Kings states:

> And Elijah said to Ahab, "Go, eat and drink, for there is the sound of a heavy rain." So Ahab went off to eat and drink, but Elijah climbed to the top of Carmel, bent down to the ground and put his face between his knees. "Go and look toward the sea," he told his servant. And he went up and looked. "There is nothing there," he said. Seven times Elijah said, "Go back." The seventh time the servant reported, "A cloud as small as a man's hand is rising from the sea." So Elijah said, "Go and tell

Ahab, 'Hitch up your chariot and go down before the rain stops you.'" Meanwhile, the sky grew black with clouds, the wind rose, a heavy rain came on and Ahab rode off to Jezreel. The power of the Lord came upon Elijah and, tucking his cloak into his belt, he ran ahead of Ahab all the way to Jezreel. (1 Kings 18.41-46, CJB)

Perhaps it is begging the issue to say that the 1 Kings text is found in the Torah, yet again it shows us proof that the source material for Ya'akov's teaching in James 5.17 of his yalqut *was the text of the Torah!*

Finally, James 5.20 notes: "...remember this: Whoever turns a sinner from the error of his way will save him from death and cover over a multitude of sins (NIV)." The concept of having sinful life patterns is stated here as αμαρτωλον...πλανης οδου αυτο (*amartolon...planes odou autou*), "a sinner (who holds to) "the error of his way." This was previously defined in this work as transgressing the instructions of the written Torah. Certainly helping to "turn a sinner" to the right life style is a concept founded in the Torah. As it is written: "Do not hate your brother in your mind. In honesty reprove your colleague, so you will not sin against him" (Leviticus 19.17, author's translation). Leviticus 19.21-22 also describes a situation in which citizens and their court system help a wayward person to turn from his Torah transgression to the proper life:

If a man sleeps with a woman who is a servant promised to another man, but who has not been ransomed or given her freedom, there must be due punishment. Yet they are not to be put to death, because she had not been freed. The man, however, must bring a ram to the entrance to the Tent of Meeting for a guilt offering to the LORD. With the ram of the guilt offering the priest is to make atonement for him before the LORD for the sin he has committed, and his sin will be forgiven" (vv.19-21, NIV, with one change by the author).

The punishment consists of the guilt offering (the אשם [*asham*]), and then forgiveness is granted from the Torah transgression. Through this process, this individual Israelite is given the opportunity to straighten out his life. This particular action is termed תשובה (*teshuvah*), "returning to God". Once again, this action a common theme in the Torah, and is part of the heart and soul of ancient and modern Jewish thought. After punishment and restitution, he can rededicate himself to keeping the instructions given in the Torah (thereby completing the process of "teshuvah"). The process described in Leviticus 19.19-21 is part of fulfilling the delicate, three-fold task proscribed in James 5.20: turning a sinner from the error of his way; saving him from death; and covering over a multitude of sins. In other words, one person attempts to encourage another to carry out the action of "teshuvah".

This again fits the theory that this yalqut comments on parashat Kedoshim. Once again we see instructions by Ya'akov that relate to the contents of this parasha. Furthermore, the idea of καλυψει πληθος αμαρτιων (*kalupsei plethos amartion*), "covering over sins", is a Torah based idea that is relayed to us here in Koine. It reflects a concept that is solidly founded

in the Torah. The phrase may be a su͏   r͏   f Torah-based
phraseology, possibly כפרת חטאים   ͏p ͏rat hata'im),
"covering of sins" or כפרת עוונות (ka   t   ͏not), or some
combination of these words (cf. Exoc   ).   Lev. 4.35, 5.6,
5.13, 5.18, 5.26, 2 Chron. 29.24, Dan   .2   My point here
is that this concept of atonement for   ns   sions, coupled
with the forgiveness of the Almighty,   ba   in the writings
of the Torah.

Chapter Five

THE CONCEPT OF
"FAITH AND WORKS"

With our understanding of Ya'akov as the Chief Rabbi of his community, and having seen his strict adherence to the teaching of the Torah, let us ask a question that often appears confusing to students of Yalqut Ya'akov. How should we understand the assertions that are made by Ya'akov in the book of James, chapter two, on the relationship between "faith and works"? I have often heard claims that Ya'akov and Sha'ul taught contradictory things about this very issue. Let us take a quick look at this subject, in light of our previously made conclusions.

First of all, we must ask what is the meaning of the word "works"(ASV), "action" (CJB) or "deeds" (NIV), as used in James 2.14, 2.17-18, 2.22, 2.24 and 2.26. Let us examine those verses:

Τι το οφελος, αδελφοι μου, εαν πιστιν λεγη τις εχειν εργα δε μη εχη; με δυναται η πιστις σωσται αυτον.

(*Ti to hophelos adelphoi mou, ean pistin lege tis hekhein erga de me ekhe; me dunatai e pistis sosai auton*).

"What good is it, my brothers, if a man claims to have faith but has no deeds? Can such faith save him?" (2.14, NIV, with the Greek word *erga* used here for "deeds"). Verses 2.17 states:

ουτως και η πιστις, εαν με εχη εργα, νεκρα εστιν καθ εαυτιν.(*Outos kai he pistis, ean me eke erga, nekra estin kath eauten*).

"In the same way, faith by itself, if it is not accompanied by action, is dead (2.17, NIV, with the word *erga* used here for "action"). James 2.18 notes:

Ἀλλ᾽ ερει τις συ πιστιν εκεις, καγω εργα εχω δειξον μοι την πιστιν σου κωρις των εργων, καγω σοι δειξω εκ των εργων μου την πιστιν. (*All erei tis su pistin ekeis, kago erga ego deikson moi ten pistin sou khoris ton ergon, kago soi deikso ek ton ergon mou τen pistin*).

"But someone will say, 'You have faith; I have deeds.' Show me your faith without deeds, and I will show you my faith by what I do" (2.18, NIV, with the Greek words *erga* and *ergon* used twice for "deeds" and "do" respectively). And again, James 2.22 states:

βλεπεις οτι η πιστις συνηργει τοις έργοις αυτου και εκ των εργον η πιστις ετελειωθη. (*Blepeis hoti he pistis sunergei tois ergois autou kai ek ton ergon he pistis heteleiothe*).

"You see that his faith and his actions were working together, and his faith was made complete by what he did" (2.22, NIV, with the Greek words ergois and *ergon* used for "actions" and "did" respectively). James 2.24 notes:

ορατε οτι εξ εργων δικαιουται ανθρωπος και ουκ εκ πιστεως μονον. (*Orote hoti eks ergon dikaioutai anthropos kai ouk ek pisteos monon*).

"You see that a person is justified by what he does and not by faith alone" (2.24, NIV, with the Greek word *ergon* used for "does"). James 2.26 teaches:

ωσπερ γαρ το σωμα κωρις πνευματος νεκρον εστιν, ουτως και η πιστις χωρις εργον νεκρα εστιν. (*Hosper gar to soma khoris pneumatos nekron estin, outos kai he pistis khoris ergon nekra estin).*

"As the body without the spirit is dead, so faith without deeds is dead" (2.26, NIV, with the Greek word *ergon* used for "deeds").

In sum, verses 2.14 and 2.17 use the Greek word *erga* for "action" or "deed". Then, *Ergois* and *ergon* (the same root words as above in 2.14 and 2.17) are used in 2.22. Finally, ergon is used again in 2.24, and again in 2.26. Thus, the same word is used in Ya'akov's yalqut when referring to all three English words: "works", "action" or "deed".

The Septuagint affords us many looks at a working definition of the word "ergon". This word, or a derivative/ conjugation of it (e.g. erga or ergois), is used in that translation of the Torah in many verses. There are multiple

83

uses of ergon/erga as the translation of the brew מעשה
(*ma'aseh*) and עשה (*'asah*)—words the xpress "an
action" and "acted/did" respectively. J rga is also
used as the translation of the Hebrew *mela'kah*),
meaning "a work of someone's hands", o ionally "a
profession". Ergon/erga is also used to ex e Hebrew
לעבוד (*la'avod*), meaning "to work". Let u ex ine a few
representative uses of "ergon/erga" in the Se agint to
illustrate this point (see glossary).

Και ειδον τον τοπον ου εισιηκει ε ι ο
θεοσ του ισραηλ και τα υπο τουσ π ασ
αυτου ωσει εργον πλινθου σαπφειρου αι
ωσπερ ειδοσ στερεωματοσ του ουρανο τη
καθαριοτητι. (*Kai eidon ton topon ou eistekei
ekei o Theos tou Israel kai ta upo tous podas autou
osei **ergon** plinthou sappheirou kai osper eidos
stereomatos tou ouranou te katharisteti*).

"...and saw the God of Israel. Under his feet was something
like a pavement made of sapphire, clear as the sky itself
(Exodus 24.10, NIV, bold emphasis is mine).

"Ergon" is used in the translation of the Hebrew phrase
כמעשה לבנת הספיר (*ke'ma'aseh livnat hasappir*), literally, "as
a work of building, or construction, or brickwork, made out
of sapphire"). In Greek, ergon is used as the cognate to the
Hebrew "ma'aseh" (work, an action of human effort).

Another example is found in Exodus 31.14:

Και φυλαξεσθε τα σαββατα οτι αγιον τουτο εστιν κυριου υμιν ο βεβηλων αυτο θανατω θανατωθησεται πασ οσ ποιησει εν αυτω εργον εξολεθρ ευθησεται η ψυχη εκεινη εκ μεσου του λαου αυτου. *(Kai phulaksesthe ta sabbata oti agion touto estin kuriou umin o bebelon a uto thanato thanatothesetai pas os poiesei en auto **ergon** eksolethr euthesetai e psukhe ekeine ek mesou tou laou autou).*

"Observe the Sabbath, because it is holy to you. Anyone who desecrates it must be put to death; whoever does any **work** on that day must be cut off from his people" (31.14, NIV, bold emphasis is mine).Here, ergon is used for the Hebrew word מְלָאכָה, (*mel'akah*), and is the word used for wage–earning work. Exodus 31.15 also provides us with a meaningful example:

Εξ ημερασ ποιησεισ εργα τη δε ημερα τη εβδομη σαββατα αναπαυσισ αγια τω κυριω πασ οσ ποιησει εργον τη ημερα τη εβδομη θανατω θανα τωθησεται. *(Eks emeras poieseis **erga** te de emera te ebdoume sabbata anapausis agia to kurio pas os poiesei **ergon** te emera te ebdoume thanato thanatouth esetai).*

"For six days, **work** is to be done, but the seventh day is a Sabbath of rest, holy to the LORD. Whoever does any **work** on the Sabbath day must be put to death" (31.15, NIV, bold emphasis is mine). Twice, in the Hebrew text of this verse, the phrase עוֹשֶׂה-מְלָאכָה (*'oseh mela'kah*), "does work", is used.

The Septuagint translated this as "poieseis erga" and "poiesei ergon". Again, the reference is to a person who carries out a wage–earning, work activity on the Sabbath. The passage, 2 Chronicles 3.10, provides another worthy example:

Και εποιησεν εν τω οικω τω αγιω των αγιων χερουβιν δυο εργον εκ ξυλ ων και εχρυσωσεν αυτα χρυσιω. (*Kai epoiesen en to oiko to agio ton agion kerouvin duo* **ergon** *ek ksulon kai ekrusosen auta krusio*).

"In the Most Holy Place he **made** a pair of sculptured cherubim and overlaid them with gold (3.10, NIV, bold emphasis mine). In this verse, ergon (in conjunction with "epoiesen") is the word used for the Hebrew phrase "vaya'as...ma'aseh", meaning "did an activity" (in this instance "handiwork", in making cherubim).

Habakkuk 1.5 provides another example:

Ιδετε οι καταφρονηται και επιβλεψατε και θαυμασατε θαυμασια και αφ ανισθητε διοτι εργον εγω εργαζομαι εν ταισ ημεραισ υμων ο ου μη πιστευσητε εαν τισ εκδιηγητα. (*Idete oi kataphronetai kai epiblepsate kai thaumasate thaumasia kai aphan isthete disti* **ergon** *ego* **ergazomai** *en tais emerais umon o ou me pisteusete ean tis ekdiegeta*).

"Look at the nations and watch, and be utterly amazed. For I am going **to do** something in your days that you would not believe, even if you were told" (1.5, NIV, bold lettering by the author). The Hebrew words פועל פועל (*fo'al po'el*) are translated into "ergazomai" and "ergon". This Hebrew verb is used to describe an action, or some type of work or initiative by a person. It is a very common, often–used word, both in Biblical and modern Hebrew. A worker or laborer is a *po'al*. Whereas, a "verb" (in Hebrew grammar) is a *po'el*, as it denotes an action. So here ergon/erga refers to an action that is taken, albeit here by the Almighty. Jeremiah 10.9 has a similar usage of erga in the context of that verse.

To state this most simply, to the translators of the Septuagint, ergon/erga denotes some type of activity or action. These are representative verses, and certainly, the many uses of ergon and erga in the Septuagint are worth a prolonged study, in and of themselves, in order to completely understand their various meanings and nuances. Nevertheless, their meanings as explained in the verses above shed some light upon our subject under discussion.

Ya'akov himself gives us an example of what an "ergon" should look like in the life of his community: "Suppose a brother or sister is without clothes and daily food, and someone says to him, '*Shalom!* Keep warm and eat hearty!' without giving him what he needs, what good does it do?" (James 2.16, CJB, italics added by translator).

Clearly the ergon, or proper "action" to take, in the above given situation is to provide clothes and food to the one who lacks it. In indicating this, Ya'akov provides us with a repetition of a mitzvah (or instruction given in the Torah). For example, the following verses, among others, could all provide the background for Ya'akov's statement: Lev. 19.18b-19, Deut.

15.7,15.10, 26.1 Isaiah 58.7,10, Ps. 10.14, Ps. 140.12, Prov. 29.7, Ezek. 22.29-31. I will repeat my assertion that Ya'akov took the very points that he has emphasized here from within the instructions of the Torah. He does not make them up and insert them into his yalqut as a new, "made up, on the spot", teaching. Therefore, in this given context, let us ask what constitutes doing an ergon (i.e. the carrying out a merciful deed)? I conclude that it is the performance of a specific set of biblical commandments.

It is clear that Ya'akov's encouragement in chapter two, to perform acts of mercy, is his call to his community to do what is written in the Torah. Indeed, Ya'akov connects his instructions to do such with the scriptural examples of Abraham (2.21-24) and Rahab (2.25). And again, the Torah is full of instructions to do the same (see above listed verses, p. 56). Then, what is it that Ya'akov implies regarding the relationship between faith, and the carrying out the mitzvot (instructions) of the Torah?

Let me first comment that the delineation between faith, as one entity, and the carrying–out of scriptural commands, as another and opposing entity, is a theologically imposed delineation that does not exist in the Jewish world. It rests on the premise that mainstream Jewish belief did not believe in salvation–by–faith; or, to put it in more Jewish terms, "entrance into the coming world was (not) based on one's trust in God." Yet, the opposite is true. I refer the reader to my book "They Loved the Torah" for an analysis of the lifestyles of Yeshua, Sha'ul, Peter, Ya'akov and the first generation of Messianic Jewish believers (see bibliography). When the emerging church in the first and second centuries abandoned many

88

Jewish modes of understanding God's kingdom, artificial categories were set up by which to interpret the scriptures. The theological belief that "justification by faith alone" is *opposed* to "fulfilling the commandments of the Torah" was one of those category sets that had an erroneous theological foundation. Yeshua's own teaching as set forth in Matthew 5.17-20, as well as his own life example to us, was abandoned in favor of spinning his teachings according to the emerging theology of the growing Gentile Church. This increased with the adoption of Christianity as the state religion of Constantine's Empire in approximately 325 A.D. But that is another story for another time. What *is* relevant to this study is what Ya'akov asserts about the relationship between faith and deeds, as found in the following verses in the book of James: "What good is it, my brothers, if a man claims to have faith but has no deeds? (2.14, NIV)...In the same way, faith by itself, if it is not accompanied by action, is dead. (2.17, NIV). But someone will say, 'You have faith; I have deeds.' Show me your faith without deeds, and I will show you my faith by what I do. (2.18, NIV)...You see that his faith and his actions were working together, and his faith was made complete by what he did. (2.22, NIV)... You see that a person is justified by what he does and not by faith alone" (2.24, NIV).

The above verses help to clarify that Ya'akov believed that fulfilling the instructions given in the Torah (i.e. "ergon", "deeds", "action", "what he does") were a certain sign of one's faith in Messiah Yeshua. The faith of this community and their ensuing fulfilling of the Torah were two parts of a whole, intrinsically connected to each other. This was true for the entire community.

89

Entire theological systems have been constructed based upon some supposed disparity between Ya'akov and Sha'ul on the issue of the meaning of "faith and works". Despite claims to the contrary, the reality is that both Ya'akov and Sha'ul held the *same* beliefs on this matter, which were consistent with second Temple Jewish belief on this same issue. As I concluded in "They Loved the Torah", it is not possible that Ya'akov was espousing an approach contrary to that of Sha'ul. Both rabbis belonged to the same Messianic Jewish community; both teachers knew of each other's work, and showed respect for it. They met with each other and Luke records a full and "Torah–honoring" cooperation between the two of them in Acts chapter 21. Organizationally, they were related to one another, and thus, worked in partnership. This is particularly true regarding Sha'ul's respect for Ya'akov, which is evident by his obedience to the request given by Ya'akov and his close circle of leaders as recorded in Acts 21.18-26. Neither is there any recorded evidence of a tete–de–tete between Ya'akov and Sha'ul on this particular issue:

> The next day Sha'ul and the rest of us went in to Ya'akov, and all the elders were present. After greeting them, Sha'ul described in detail each of the things God had done among the Gentiles through his efforts. On hearing it, they praised God; but they also said to him, "You see, brother, how many tens of thousands of believers there are among the Judeans, and they are all zealots for the *Torah*. Now what they have been told about you is that you are teaching all the Jews living among

the *Goyim* to apostatize from Moshe, telling them not to have a *b'rit-milah* for their sons and not to follow the traditions. "What, then, is to be done? They will certainly hear that you have come. So, do what we tell you. We have four men who are under a vow. Take them with you, be purified with them, and pay the expenses connected with having their heads shaved. Then everyone will know that there is nothing to these rumors, which they have heard about you; but that, on the contrary, you yourself stay in line and keep the *Torah*. "However, in regard to the *Goyim* who have come to trust in Yeshua, we all joined in writing them a letter with our decision that they should abstain from what had been sacrificed to idols, from blood, from what is strangled and from fornication." The next day Sha'ul took the men, purified himself along with them and entered the Temple to give notice of when the period of purification would be finished and the offering would have to be made for each of them (Acts 21.18-26, CJB, italics are added by the translator).

These eight verses clearly relay the great respect which Sha'ul had for Ya'akov, and the acceptance, on behalf of Sha'ul, of the authority of Ya'akov. Likewise, Ya'akov respected Sha'ul, as evidenced in Acts 15.4, 12, as he listens to Sha'ul's experiences and conclusions, and agrees with them as recorded in chapter 15.13-20. This occurs about 45-50 CE. Additionally, Ya'akov's respect for Sha'ul is demonstrated through evidence of his acceptance of the life–work of Sha'ul, proven later in Acts: "The next day Paul and the rest of us went to see James, and all the elders were present. Paul greeted them and reported in detail what God had done among the Gentiles through his ministry. When they heard this, they praised God" (21.18b-20, NIV, approximately 60 CE, about two years before the deaths of both Sha'ul and Ya'akov). Indeed, "James gave Paul the right hand of fellowship and endorsed his mission to the Gentiles." [1] Much of Sha'ul's "mission" to the Gentiles consisted of teaching and writing that upheld the decisions of the Messianic Jewish Sanhedrin as relayed by Acts 15. As Ya'akov presided over these decisions, Sha'ul and Ya'akov were certainly agreed in its content. Acts 15 gives absolutely no evidence to the contrary.

Ya'akov's teaching in chapter two is thoroughly consistent with a Jewish understanding of how one's faith affects his life, in other words, that a sincere follower of Israel's God will always be fulfilling the Torah's commandments. Instead of viewing these two elements in conceptual juxtaposition to each other, Ya'akov saw them as working hand in hand with each other. The keeping of the Torah's commandments was inherently connected to the life and mindset of anyone who believed in Israel's God. The motivation to fulfill those instructions that in particular help other people with their needs flowed from both the injunctions of the Torah text, and from the community's relationship to their Holy Rabbi Yeshua, their Messiah. "James was 'Torah true' and believed in righteous deeds as an important part of being a follower of Jesus." [2] Of course Ya'akov believed that עשיית המצוות (Hebrew, *asiyat ha-mitzvot*) "the *doing* of the mitzvoth," which is fulfilling the biblical commands, was an important part of being a student of the Holy Rabbi Yeshua. *Any* other approach would have been a radical departure from the given Jewish norm of that era, as well as a radical deviation from the teachings of Yeshua himself (cf. Matthew 5.17ff).

As Shanks and Witherington state, "James (Ya'akov) was certainly an observant Jew throughout his life, and he never strayed from this orientation. He believed Jewish followers of Jesus should be obligated to faithfully observe the Law." [3] It is beyond the scope of this book to expound on my next point in sufficient depth, but let me simply state that the entire leadership of the early Jerusalem Messianic Jewish community (including Sha'ul) were also observant Jews throughout their entire lifetimes. I cover this particular point in detail in my work "They Loved the Torah".

The lifestyle of Yeshua's students was set by him and by generations of devout Jews before him. It consisted of keeping the biblical commandments as a foundation, as part–and–parcel of who they were. It constituted a vital part of what it meant to belong to Ya'akov's community of Messianic Jews. This is an historically consistent reality. Observing the Torah was central to the life of all of Israel in Ya'akov's day, and has been so throughout history till today. The Torah was regarded as the purveyor of life, as the Heavenly blueprint for human life, and as the communicator of truth for the entire Jewish people worldwide, from Ya'akov's day down until today.

TABLE ONE

TABLE OF COMPARISONS: YALKUT and MASEKET

Yalqut Ya'akov (circa. 60 c.e.) and Maseket Avot (150 b.c.e.-200 c.e.) contain similar subjects and contents. The following table is a self-study for the reader by which to compare these two sets of teachings. I acknowledge the prior work of Dr. Walter Kaiser in compiling his comparative table on this same book between Yalqut Ya'akov and the book of Leviticus.

Subject	Yalqut Ya'akov	Pirke Avot
1. The poor	2.1-7	1.5,11
2. Proper speech	3.2-11	1.5
3. Judging others	4.11-12	1.6, 2.5
4. Bragging, pompousness, self-assurance, pride	4.14-16	1.10 ("rabbanut","רבנות")
5. Attitudes & anger	1.19-20	1.15, 2.15, 4.1
6. "ha-ma'aseh" (applying Torah)	2.21-26	2.17, 3.12, 3.22
7. "torah transgression causes more torah transgression"	2.10-11	4.2
8. humbleness	2.17-20, 4.6,10	4.4, 4.6, 4.12-13

TABLE TWO

TABLE OF COMPARSIONS:
THE ROLES OF THE RELEVANT CHIEF RABBIS

NASI	RESH GALUTA	YA'AKOV
Presided over Sanhedrin/	Presided over court system/	Presided over community's court system
Ordained scholars/	Ordained scholars/	Ordained scholars
(that is, scholars were ordained in their community, under their supervision)		
Communicated with galut	Communicated with galut	Communicated with galut
Dispatched shalihim:	Dispatched shalihim:	Dispatched shalihim:
Taught, set up courts, raised funds	Taught, set up courts, raised funds	Taught, set up courts, raised funds
Legislated halakha	Legislated halakha	Legislated halakha
Descendant of David (and Hillel)	Descendant of David	Descendant of David
Recorded teachings: in the Mishna and Gemara	Recorded teachings: in the Gemara	Recorded teachings: in book of Yakov & Acts
Depended upon voluntary cooperation to function	Depended upon voluntary cooperation to function	Depended upon voluntary cooperation to function

We can conclude from history that Ya'akov's role had major parallels to the Nasi of the Great Sanhedrin of his era. Conceptual parallels also existed between Yakov's role and that of the Resh Galuta. All three roles described above were community leadership roles of a rabbinic, halakhic and political nature that dealt with jurisprudence and the formation of halakha, among other things.

95

TABLE THREE

LISTING OF THE NASI'IM (Chief Rabbis) OF THE GREAT SANHEDRIN

(Taken from: http://www.middleeastexplorer.com/Israel/Na

Nasi	Start of role (date)	Finish of role (date)
Unknown	191 BCE	170 BCE
Yose ben Yoezer	170 BCE	140 BCE
Joshua ben Perachyah	140 BCE	100 BCE
Simeon ben Shetach	100 BCE	60 BCE
Sh'maya	65 BCE	c. 31 BCE
Hillel the Elder	c. 31 BCE	9 CE
Rabban Shimon ben Hillel	9	9
Rabban Gamaliel the Elder	9	50
Rabban Shimon ben Gamliel	50	80
Rabban Gamaliel II of Yavne	80	118
Rabbi Eleazar ben Azariah	118	120
Interregnum (Bar Kokhba revolt)	120	142
Rabban Shimon ben Gamliel II	142	165
Rabbi Judah I haNasi	165	220
Gamaliel III	220	230
Judah II Nesi'ah	230	270
Gamaliel IV	270	290
Judah III Nesi'ah	290	320
Hillel II	320	365
Gamliel V	365	385
Judah IV	385	400
Gamaliel VI--murdered	c. 400	425

TABLE FOUR

MESSIANIC JEWISH "NASI'IM"
OF THIS EARLY COMMUNITY

Nasi	Start of role (date)	Finish of role (date)
Ya'akov ben Yosef	33	62
Shimon	62	?
Justus	?	?
Zakiah	?	?
Tuvya	?	?
Binyamin	?	?
Yohanan	?	?
Matityahu	?	?
Philip	?	?
Seneca	?	?
Justus II	?	?
Levi	?	?
Ephres	?	?
Yosef	?	?
Yehudah	?	135

This list is provided by the historian Eusebius (d. 339 a.d.). He finishes his listing by noting: "…that was the number of bishops in the city of Jerusalem from apostolic times to the date mentioned (i.e. 135 a.d.), all of them of the Circumcision."[4]

Readily apparent is that Hadrian's expulsion of the Jewish community of Jerusalem ended, at least from Eusebius' knowledge, the line of "nasi" leadership in the Messianic Jewish community. Secondly, historical knowledge of these aforementioned men—their biographies, accomplishments as chief rabbis, etc., is sketchy, at best.

97

ENDNOTES

Foreword

1. Stern, D. H. 1989. *Jewish New Testament : A translation of the New Testament that expresses its Jewishness* (1st ed.) . Jewish New Testament Publications: Jerusalem, Israel; Clarksville, Md., USA

Introduction

1. By "halakhic", I mean Jewish jurisprudence. This meant that the halakhic council or court that Ya'akov headed developed community practices based upon their understanding of the commandments of the Torah (cf. Acts 15; notice Ya'akov's role as chief judge of this halakhic court).

2. In his "Church History", Book IV, Chapter V, we find Eusebius' list of chief rabbis in the ancient Jerusalem Messianic Jewish community.

Chapter One

1. A. Hauser and D. Watson, *A History of Biblical Interpretation* (Grand Rapids, MI: Eerdmans Publications, 2009),134.

2. Modern scholarship has debated whether Mishnaic (Middle) Hebrew or Aramaic was the spoken language of the Land of Israel in the first century. Along with Bivin and Blizzard's conclusions, I stand with the Jerusalem School of Synoptic Research, who argues for Mishnaic Hebrew. Although I affirm many of Shanks and Witherington's (see bibliography) conclusions regarding Ya'akov, I firmly disagree with their assertion for Aramaic as the daily spoken language of first century Israel. My research affirms that the native language was Hebrew, though Aramaic was spoken and read by a good amount of the population, as was Greek. Ya'akov's weekly parasha, or Torah lessons, served as the equivalent of today's "shi'ur" from a community rabbi —that is, his parasha highlighted teaching on a section of the Torah.

3. Doron Mendels, "Why Paul Went West," *BAR,* 37, no.1 (2011): 45.

4. Daniel Gruber shares interesting insights on "Jewish Greek" in his work "Copernicus and the Jews," pp. 18–37, chapter entitled Parlez-vous Jewish Greek?" (See bibliography).

5. Daniel B. Wallace, "James: Introduction, Outline and Argument." *Bible.org.* http://bible.org/seriespage/james-introduction-outline-and-argument. (accessed 6 November, 2011).

6. Shanks and Witherington affirm the same point in their work (see bibliography), pp. 143–145.

7. Shanks and Witherington, *The Brother of Jesus* (San Francisco, CA: Harper, 2003),144.

8. Hauser and Watson, *A History of Biblical Interpretation,* 134.

9. That is, the *Mekilta d'Rabbi Yishmael*, an edition of midrash on the book of Exodus. One may consult the Jewish Publication Society's edition, edited by Jacob Lauterbach. See bibliography.

10. Dunn is quoted by A. Selvaggio in "Hearing the Voice of Jesus in the Epistle of James" (see bibliography).

11. Too often, it is assumed that the first century Messianic Jews somehow rejected the importance of carrying out the *mitzvot* of the Torah (the Biblical commandments) in lieu of having faith in the Messiah. That is, they exchanged one for the other. This erroneous belief is well countered by Ya'akov's continued emphasis on how one's faith in Messiah is primarily evidenced *by one's keeping of the commandments.* Shimon ben Gamliel's teaching: *"ve'lo hamidrash hu ha'ikar, elah hama'aseh"*, "the principal matter is not study (of the Torah), but practice" (Pirke Avot 1.17) is repeated in the teaching of Ya'akov. It is also of note that Shimon was a contemporary of Ya'akov. The book of James affirms the extant Jewish viewpoint of "the affirmation cited in Exodus (24:7): 'when the people heard the covenant of the Torah they responded, "All that the L-rd has spoken we will do and we will hear."' First action, then study" (Rieser, p. 38). Ya'akov writes in such a way as to promote this priority. In fact, in my estimation, only a few verses of his book deal directly with

faith encouragement (e.g. 1.3), whereas the six final verses of chapter 1 and all twenty-six verses of chapter 2 deal directly with encouraging the performance of the Biblical commandments. In fact, verses 2.18–26 let us know, in no uncertain terms, that faith in the Messiah *must* be expressed by the carrying out of the mitzvot.

Chapter Two

1. My educated guess is that Ya'akov spoke these words as part of his *parasha* lesson, and his students memorized his oral teaching. At some point afterwards, his teaching was written down and then spread in the Messianic Jewish world. I have no doubt that Ya'akov gave this lesson in Mishnaic Hebrew, and that it was subsequently translated into Greek (as we have it today) for use among Greek speaking Messianic Jews in the Diaspora.

2. See Sanhedrin 37a ("According to this, man was created alone, to teach you that anyone who destroys a single person from Israel, the Written Torah likens him to one who destroyed a full world; but he who saves one person of Israel, the Written Torah likens him to one who saved a full world," author's translation). The idiom used here for "saves" (from the Hebrew word לקיים, *leqayem*) can mean *to correctly interpret and teach the Torah* (italics mine). Thus this Mishnah may be teaching us that if one teaches the Torah correctly, he "saves" people in Israel, and if he teaches wrongly, he destroys his fellow Jews.

3. "Logically," in that Ya'akov was probably the flesh and blood, half-brother of Yeshua, as well as his devoted student. Thus, it is fitting to assume that the theological bearings and conclusions of the rabbi would be those of his brother and student. Shanks and Witherington devote pp. 146–152 of their work "The Brother of Jesus" to this very point.

4. I translated the idiom "*talmud torah*" (תלמוד תורה) from Avot 6.2 as "acquisition of Torah", by which I mean both learning its texts and also practicing it as a community lifestyle.

5. Daniel Gruber, *The Messianic Writings* (Hanover, NH: Elijah Press, 2011), n.p.

6. Robert Alter writes on this very point in his work "The Art of Biblical Narrative," 94–95 (See bibliography).

7. Nosson Weisz, "We will do and we will hear (Na'aseh V'Nishma)," *aish.com,* May 14, 2002 (accessed on 22 January 2012). http://aish.com/h/sh/se/48967001.html.

8. Parasha study was not, and is not, restricted only to Sabbaths, but it is a focus on Sabbaths.

9. In Ya'akov's lifetime, the parasha cycle in Israel was probably a three year cycle, not a one year cycle, as is extant today. The particular parasha under discussion may not have carried the name *Kedoshim* in the first century, as it does today. There was a like need for both of these books in their given generations that may explain some of the similarity that they share.

Chapter Three

1. By *halakha,* I mean a community standard based upon interpretation of the Torah, and decided upon by the community's authoritative body. Such was clearly lacking before 50AD.

2. See "Binding and Loosing", *Jewish Encyclopedia,* Available from http://www.jewishencyclopedia.com/articles/3307-binding-and-loosing.

3. *Talmid hakam* is Hebrew for "wise student", referring to the chief, most learned, or most mature, student of a given rabbi's inner circle. Please see my chapter "Simon Peter, Yeshua's special student." pp. 59–65 in 'They Loved the Torah' (see bibliography).

4. Cornelius is described as a God fearer (cf. Acts 10.2, *phobomenos,* φοβομενος), and Lydia is as well (cf. Acts 16.14, *sebomene,* σεβουμενη). This category included Gentiles who were already carefully keeping much of the Torah, as well as many Jewish customs and the Jewish religious calendar, without undergoing formal conversion.

5. In terms of its intended longevity, it is my opinion that these points have never been changed; this halakha remains intact. In terms of being faithfully practiced by Gentile believers, this halakha is not often studied with current validity given to its contents.

6. I am identifying Shaul as a prominent member of the Jerusalem-based Messianic Jewish community, sent out from them to share about the Messiah in foreign nations. But this is the subject of a whole separate study.

7. I am grateful to Mr. Aryeh Powlison of Jerusalem, Israel for drawing my attention to the Greek phrasing here, over 25 years ago.

8. H. Freedman, "Introduction," Tractate Nedarim, http://www.come-and-hear.com/nedarim/index.html (accessed 5 March, 2011).

9. Shanks and Witherington affirm this practice in the early Messianic Jewish community, and discuss it in p. 113 of their work (see bibliography).

10. This does not imply that the Acts 15 halakhic decision was made by Ya'akov alone. He summarized and communicated this crucial halakhic decision. In addition, the implementation of this decision was done with much struggle, one that Shaul engaged in often (e.g. the book of Galatians was written as part of his personal struggle to implement these decisions in that region. Again, that is a subject for a different essay).

11. Yosef ben Mattityahu, a.k.a. Josephus, was a younger contemporary of Ya'akov, dying in approximately 100AD. His recollections of Ya'akov may be quite accurate, given his proximity in time and location. I do recognize, as have historians who have chronicled the contributions of ben Mattityahu (such as Steven Mason), that his writings were not free from manipulations and prejudices. (On the other hand, most historians show these same characteristics, especially ancient historians).

12. A careful study of Newer Testament narratives shows us that the Pharisees were *not*, as a party, the wholesale enemies of Yeshua, nor of Ya'akov (cf. Acts 23.6-9, where Pharisees come to Shaul's defense; and Luke 13.31, where Pharisees attempt to tip off Yeshua about Antipas' plot to murder him). The Sadducees (such as Hananya [Ananus in the quoted text]) were much more antagonistic, and their leadership was involved along with the Roman occupation forces in killing Yeshua. Ben Mattityahu fingers the Sadducean leadership for the murder of Ya'akov. On the other hand, Hegesippus blames at least one group of Pharisees!

13. Hegesippus, "Commentaries on tl A   the Church," http.//
earlychristianwritings/text/hegesippus/html cc   ! February, 2012).

14. . "*Sadiq*" is Hebrew for a "righteous   In Second Temple
times, it was a technical term for a scrupulously   observant person.
Joseph, the father of Yeshua, is called by a cognate t m   Greek ("*dikaios*"
in Matthew 1.19), as is Shimon (see Luke 2.25; a   in "*dikaios*" is used).
Netanel (Nathaniel), to whom Yeshua spoke in John   5-48, is inferred as
being in such a category of person as well. I am p   ig the Greek term
"*dikaios*" to the Hebrew "*sadiq*", which parallel   tten about in my
work "They Loved the Torah" (see bibliography).

15. Hegesippus, "Commentaries on the Acts of   Church," http.//
earlychristianwritings/text/hegesippus/html? (2 Febr   012).

16. Ibid.

17. Ibid.

18. Shanks and Witherington, 156 and 94.

19. Again, the role of *nasi* bore similarities to a Chief   tice of the
US Supreme Court, combined with being a Chief rabbi of th ommunity.
Av bet din was the functional head of Sanhedrin meetings a combined
sergeant-at-arms and Speaker of the House, as well as a leading rabbi-
scholar). Rabban Gamliel was the teacher of Shaul the Pharisee.

20. Shanks and Witherington, 162.

21. I include the entire believing community in Yeshua here, both
within the Land of Israel, and in the Diaspora lands.

22. Shanks and Witherington, 162.

23. Ibid.

Chapter Four

1. Gruber, page not specified. Kindle Locations 78-79.

3. I refer the reader to *The Sage in Israel and the ancient Near East* by
John G. Gammie and Leo Perdue, p. 330ff, for a discussion of the contents
of Hellenist "wisdom", as well as "Greek popular morality in the time of
Plato and Aristotle" by K.J. Dover, p. 58, for his quick analysis of the
use of the word "sophos", and finally "The Sophists" by W.K. Chambers-
Guthrie, p. 27ff).

3. One of the author's favorite comments on interpreting the Torah was made by Rabbi Naftali Zvi Yehudah Berlin, the renowned "Netziv" (d. 1893), who commented that all of the Torah can be seen as a book of Hebrew poetry. I remain very appreciative of this perspective in looking at the emphases and flow of the text of the Torah.

4. The italics are taken from the website that is quoted:

http://www.stfonline.org/pdf/rev/appendix%20b_commentary.pdf

5. Josephus, *Wars of the Jews,* ii.15, pgh.1.

6. Shanks and Witherington, p. 113. Although this author is not convinced that Ya'akov took a lifelong Nazirite vow, the use of Nazirite vows within the original Messianic Jewish community in 1st century Jerusalem is attested to by Shanks and Witherington.

Chapter Five

1. Shanks and Witherington, p. 215.

2. Ibid., p. 113.

3. Ibid., p. 215

4. Eusebius, The History of the Church from Christ to Constantine, p. 145.

GLOSSARY

Admor: A Hebrew title of honor; short for "our master, our teacher and our rabbi".

Adonai: One of the Hebrew names for 'God'.

Aggadah (and its adjective, aggadic; its plural form is aggadot): Rabbinic literature that is of a narrative, story telling nature that makes a moral, ethical point, or offers commentary to help understand religious writings.

Av: Literally, a "father". In Jewish biblical interpretation, it refers to a general category or principle for either categorizing or interpreting the Torah.

Av bet din: Literally, 'father of the court.' This role referred to one of the two chief rabbis of the Great Sanhedrin.

Avtalyon: One of the two leading Sanhedrin teachers in the generation prior to Hillel and Shammai. He was the partner of Shemaiah (see below).

Bar Mitzvah: the time when a Jewish youth becomes responsible for keeping the Torah. This occurs at age 13 for boys, and is marked by their first public reading from the Torah.

Berakhot: One of the tractates of the Babylonian Talmud.

Chief rabbi: Though not an official title in the 1st century as it is today, I have chosen this term to parallel that of the 'nasi' of the Great Sanhedrin, and I use it to encompass the role that Yakov filled in his era.

Diaspora: The exile of Jewish communities who lived outside the land of Israel in history. In other words, any Jewish community outside of Israel is in the diaspora.

Dibah: a category of forbidden speech in Judaism, akin to the category of slander in modern western jurisprudence.

Galut: Hebrew for diaspora (see its above definition).

Haggadah: The written text used for guiding families through the Passover meal.

Halakha (or *halakhic*): Applications of the biblical commandments to a community lifestyle.

Hillel: A 1st century sage who was the Nasi of the Sanhedrin in his era; one of the founders of the Pharisees.

Hoq: A type of written commandment in the Bible. In this essay, used in reference to "hoq herut", that is, the 'law of liberty' as referred to by Yakov.

Hose'et shem ra: The act of telling an untrue fact about someone to others in order to influence their opinion toward said person, or affect their actions towards said person.

Kedusha: God's holiness, which is at once powerful and healing, which breaks mightily into human history at various times, and will particularly do so in a permanent way in the world to come.

Koine: The name for the Second Temple era, Greek lingua franca that was used across the Mediterranean world.

Kvitel: A written note of supplication to God, left at the grave of renowned rabbi.

Lashon hara: The act of speaking negatively about someone else to influence another's opinion, whether the facts relayed are true or untrue.

Matza: Hebrew for unleavened bread.

Mekilta d'Rabbi Yishmael: A famous ancient midrashic work on the book of Exodus.

Messianic Jews (or *Messianic Jewish*): As used in this essay, the original Jewish believers in Jesus from the first century time period, with its ancient flagship community in Jerusalem.

Midrash (and its adjective, *midrashic*): A type of rabbinic commentary that plays off the literal text, in attempting to explain it. The midrash usually, but not always, is of a storytelling nature that explains the given biblical text.

Mishna: A section of teaching and commentary in the earlier portion of the Talmud; this word is also used to describe the entire earlier portion of the Talmud (redacted in approximately 200 a.d.).

Mitzvot: The biblical commandments. This can also refer to merciful actions.

Musar: A 19th and 20th century religious movement within Eastern European Judaism, founded by Rabbi Y. Salanter, that emphasized the study of ethical teachings.

Nasi: The role of Chief Justice of the Sanhedrin (in both the Great Sanhedrin of 71 judges, and in the sanhedrin of Messianic Jewish leaders found in Acts 15).

Parasha: The weekly scripture portions that are studied in the Jewish world, from ancient times until today.

Parashat Kedoshim or *Kedoshim*: One of the parasha portions from the book of Leviticus, usually studied in the late winter or early springtime.

Pirke Avot: Also known as 'Ethics of the Fathers', this is a book of summary teachings of Tannaitic (and earlier) teachers. It is part of the Mishna.

Rabbinic responsa: Letters written by rabbinic authorities in response to questions of halakhic practice in various communities. Shaul's epistles for the most part fit into this literary-religious category.

Sadiq: Hebrew for 'righteous', this term refers to a scrupulously Torah observant person or a particularly pious religious leader. In Hasidic and Yiddish usage, the word is enunciated more as "tsaddik", though it is the same word.

Sanhedrin: Hebrew (from Greek) for a body of judges who deliberate on halakhic issues. A Sanhedrin could range from 3 judges to the Great Sanhedrin in Jerusalem, which included 71 judges, and ruled only on cases of supreme importance, akin in some ways to the Supreme Court of some nations today. Sanhedrins existed as local, village- centered courts, as well as in more urban areas.

Sara: A forbidden category of speech in Jewish jurisprudence, perhaps a type of slander or libel.

Septuagint: The Greek translation of the Hebrew Bible, done in the 3rd century b.c., in order to help Egyptian Jews understand the scriptures.

Shammai: Served on the Sanhedrin as one of its top leaders, judges and teachers, along with Hillel (see listing under Hillel).

Shmaayah (or *Shemaiah*): A top Sanhedrin leader in the generation preceding that of Hillel and Shammai.

Shaul: The original Hebrew name of Paul of Tarsus.

Shi'urim: Hebrew for 'lessons', in this essay specifically referring to weekly Torah lessons given by Yakov to his community.

Takkanah: A rabbinic law, halakhic decision or custom that is made in order to enable fulfillment of the biblical commandments.

Talmid Hakam: "Wise student" in Hebrew, it refers to the role of the chief student of a rabbi. This was a role of responsibility, and one of modeling to the other students. The *talmid hakam* was expected to carry on the teachings of his rabbi after the latter's demise.

Tenach: The Bible, in the context of this essay referring to Genesis-Malachi.

Teshuvah: The process of repentance.

Ya'akov: The original Hebrew name of James 'the Just', the subject of this essay.

Yalqut: A compendium or collection of writings or teachings. These are often the highlighted Torah commentaries of a given rabbi, scholar or commentator.

In some popular spellings, it is spelled "yalkut".

Yeshua: The original Hebrew name of Jesus.

Yosef: The original Hebrew name of the 1st century historian Josephus (in Hebrew, *Yosef* ben Matityahu).

BIBLIOGRAPHY

Adler, Aaron. "Prerequisites for the First Commandment." YBA Parsha Thoughts. Accessed 6 March, 2011. http://www.afyba. org/parsha.asp?parashaId=238&archive=yes.

Aland, Kurt and Nestle, Erwin, eds. Novum Testamentum Graece. Stuttgart, Germany: Deutsche Bibelstiftung, 1979.

Alter, Robert. The Art of Biblical Narrative. N.Y., NY: Basic Books, 2011.

Avoda. "Boil it down for me." The Jewish Service Corps, publishers. Accessed 1 August, 2011. http://www.avodah.net/assets/ Weekly-Torah-Teachings/Bamidbar-Numbers/7-146- Balak-Boil-it-Down-for-Me.

Ben Mattityahu, Yosef. The Wars of the Jews, Book II. Accessed 4 October, 2011. http://www.sacred-texts.com/jud/josephus/ war-2.htm.

Buth, Randall. "The Book of James: A Positive View of the Law." Presentation, Jerusalem, Israel, March 8, 1997.

Buttrick, George, ed. The Interpreter's Bible. Nashville, TN: Abingdon-Cokesbury, 1952.

Casper, Bernard. An Introduction to Jewish Bible Commentary. N.Y., NY: Yoseloff, 1960.

Chabad.org library. Ethics of the Fathers. Accessed 7 November, 2011. http://www.chabad.org/library/article_cdo/ aid2165/jewish/Chapter-One.htm.

111

Chambers-Guthrie, W.K.G. The Sophists. Cambridge, U.K.: Camgridge University Press, 1969.

Danizier, D. "Paul v. James." Accessed 1 March 2012. http://www.wordwiz72.com/paul.html

Dillenberger, John, editor. Martin Luther: Selections From His Writings. Garden City, NY: Doubleday Publishers, 1961.

Dover, K.J. Greek Popular Morality in the Time of Plato and Aristotle. Cambridge, MA: Hackett Publishers, 1994.

Eusebius. The History of the Church from Christ to Constantine. Baltimore, MD: Penguin Books Ltd., 1967.

Fischer, P. "Modern Day God-Fearers: A Biblical Role Model for Gentile Participation in Messianic Congregations." The Enduring Paradox: Exploratory Essays in Messianic Judaism. Edited by John Fischer. Baltimore: Lederer/Messianic Jewish Publishers. (2000): 171–181.

Freedman, H. "Introduction." Tractate Nedarim. Accessed March 5, 2011. http://www.come-and-hear.com/nedarim/index.html.

Friedman, David. They Loved the Torah. Baltimore, MD: Lederer Books, 2001.

_____. Bereshit: The Book of Beginnings. Eugene, OR: Wipf and Stock, 2010.

Gammie, John G. and Perdue, Leo, eds. The Sage in Israel and the ancient Near East. Winona Lake, IN: Eisenbrauns, 1990.

Gannon, Kassiani. e-mail message to author. January 2012.

Grant, Michael. The Jews in the Roman World. N.Y., NY: Barnes and Noble Books, 1995.

"Greek Text of the Book of James." Accessed 2 March, 2011. http://www.bookofjames.info/greek.html.

Gruber, D. Copernicus and the Jews. Hanover, N.H.: Elijah Publishing, 2005.

_____. The Messianic Writings. Hanover, N.H.: Elijah Publishing, 2011.

Gruber, I. interview by author. September 2011, Jerusalem, Israel.

112

Hauser, A. and Watson, D. A History of Biblical Interpretation: The Medieval through the Reformation Periods. Grand Rapids, MI: Eerdmans Publications, 2009.

Hegessipus. "Commentaries on the Acts of the Church." Accessed 2 February, 2012. http://www.earlychristianwritings.com/text/hegesippus.html.

Hemed Publishers. Maseket Sanhedrin. Jerusalem, Israel, 1978.

Jewish Encyclopedia. "Binding and Loosing." Accessed 20 February, 2012. http://www.jewishencyclopedia.com/articles/3307-binding-and-loosing.

Johnson, Luke T. "The Use of Leviticus 19 in the Letter of James." Journal of Biblical Literature 101 (1982): 301–401.

Kaiser, Walter. "James' View of the Law," Mishkan 8/9 (1988): 9–12.

Kinzer, Mark. Israel's Messiah and the People of God. Eugene, OR: Wipf and Stock, 2011.

Koren Publishers. Torah, Nevi'im, Ketuvim. Jerusalem, Israel: Koren.

"Makkot 23b-24a." Accessed 5 November 2011. http://www.avodah.net/assets/Weekly-Torah-Teachings/Bamidbar-Numbers/7-146-Balak-Boil-it-Down-for-Me.

Mason, Steve. Josephus and the New Testament. Ada, MI: Baker Publishing Group, 2002.

Mendels, Doron. "Why Paul Went West." Biblical Archaeology Review 37, no. 1 (2011): 49–54. https://www.bibarch.org/bar/article.asp?PubID=BSBA&Volume=37&Issue.

"Nasi." Accessed 5 October, 2011. http://www.middleeastexplorer.com/Israel/Nasi.

Reiser, Louis. "On One Foot: An In-Depth Analysis of B. Shabbat 30b–31a." CCAR Journal: A Reform Jewish Quarterly Fall/W (2003): 30–50.

Safrai, S. and Stern, M., eds. The Jewish People in the First Century, Volumes I and II. Minneapolis, MN: VanGorcum. Fortress Press, 1976.

Scherman, Nosson, trans. and commentator. The Complete Art Scroll Siddur. Brooklyn, NY: Mesorah Publications, 1984.

Schonfield, Hugh. The History of Jewish Christianity. (No further information given).

Selvaggio, Anthony. "Hearing the Voice of Jesus in the Epistle of James." Accessed 3 November, 2011. http://www.reformation21.org/articles/hearing-the-voice-of-jesus-in-the-epistle-of-james.php.

Shanks, H. and Witherington, B. The Brother of Jesus. San Francisco, CA: Harper, 2003.

"Shabbat 31." Accessed 7 January 2012. http://come-and-hear.com/shabbath/shabbath_31.html.

Study Light Organization, eds. The Adam Clarke Commentary. 10 February, 2011. http://www.studylight.org/com/acc/view.cgi?book=jas&chapter=002.

"The Greek Words for Prayer." Accessed 3 October, 2011. http://www.stfonline.org/pdf/rev/appendix%20b_commentary.pdf.

Tabor, James. "Ancient Judaism: Josephus on James." Accessed 3 March, 2011. http://religiousstudies.uncc.edu/people/jtabor/james.html.

"Tractate Shabbat." Soncino Talmud Online. Accessed 22 January, 2012. http://halakhah.com/pdf/moed/Shabbath.pdf.

Wallace, Daniel. "James: Introduction, Outline and Argument." Bible.org. Accessed 6 November, 2011. http://bible.org/seriespage/james-introduction-outline-and-argument.

Weisz, Nosson. "We will do and we will hear." Accessed 22 January, 2012. http://www.aish.com/h/sh/se/48967001.html.

"Yalkut Shimoni." Accessed 12 January, 2011. http://www.tsel.org/torah/yalkutsh/index.html.

Disclaimer: author assumes no responsibility for changes in, or removal of, cited website addresses.

AUTHOR BIOGRAPHY

Dr. David Friedman is the former Academic Dean and Professor of Jewish Studies at King of Kings College in Jerusalem, Israel. He is the author of numerous books and articles, including They Loved the Torah, Sudden Terror, Who Knows Abba Arika, and Bereshit, the Book of Beginnings. Currently, Friedman lectures internationally on biblical topics, as well as on the history of the modern State of Israel. He also works actively in the area of Jewish-Arab reconciliation as a speaker and mentor, and is an advocate for a secure State of Israel. He is a former member of the IDF - Israel Defense Forces. His work as a college lecturer included pioneering a unique course on the history of the Holocaust, where he regularly brought his students to Eastern Europe for on-site instruction. Friedman was ordained with the first class of UMJC rabbis and was a teacher in the UMJC yeshiva educational program. While resident in the USA, he was an NCAA baseball coach, as well as a high school baseball coach. He is married, with adult children and two grandchildren.

CONTRIBUTING AUTHOR BIOGRAPHY

B.D. Friedman is a native and resident of Jerusalem, Israel. He is a student and researcher in Ancient Hebrew and Biblical topics. Currently he writes a monthly column, translating the Bible from Hebrew into "easy to be understood" English. Recently, Friedman has taught Biblical studies in Ireland and in the Netherlands. This represents his first collaboration on writing a book.

OTHER RELATED RESOURCES

Available at Messianic Jewish Resources Int'l. • www.messianicjewish.net
1-800-410-7367
(Prices subject to change.)

Coming Soon! ### Complete Jewish Study Bible - New Testament

- The New Testament portion of the Complete Jewish Bible, adapted for the American audience.
- Introductions and articles by well known Messianic Jewish theologians including Dr. David Friedman, Dr. John Fischer, Dr. Jeffrey Seif, Dr. Dan Juster, Rabbi Russ Resnik, and more.
-Hebrew Idioms found in the New Testament explained by Israeli Messianic Jewish scholar, Dr. David Friedman.

Complete Jewish Bible: *A New English Version*
—Dr. David H. Stern

Presenting the Word of God as a unified Jewish book, the *Complete Jewish Bible* is a new version for Jews and non-Jews alike. It connects Jews with the Jewishness of the Messiah, and non-Jews with their Jewish roots. Names and key terms are returned to their original Hebrew and presented in easy-to-understand transliterations, enabling the reader to say them the way Yeshua (Jesus) did! 1697 pages.

Hardback	**JB12**	$34.99
Paperback	**JB13**	$29.99
Leather Cover	**JB15**	$59.99
Large Print (12 Pt font)	**JB16**	$49.99

Also available in French and Portuguese.

Jewish New Testament
—Dr. David H. Stern

The New Testament is a Jewish book, written by Jews, initially for Jews. Its central figure was a Jew. His followers were all Jews; yet no other version really communicates its original, essential Jewishness. Uses neutral terms and Hebrew names. Highlights Jewish references and corrects mistranslations. Freshly translated into English from Greek, this is a must read to learn about first-century faith. 436 pages

Hardback	**JB02**	$19.99
Paperback	**JB01**	$14.99
Spanish	**JB17**	$24.99

Also available in French, German, Polish, Portuguese and Russian.

Jewish New Testament Commentary
—Dr. David H. Stern

This companion to the *Jewish New Testament* enhances Bible study. Passages and expressions are explained in their original cultural context. 15 years of research. 960 pages.

Hardback	**JB06**	$34.99
Paperback	**JB10**	$29.99

Jewish New Testament on Audio CD or MP3

All the richness of the *Jewish New Testament* beautifully narrated in English by professional narrator/singer, Jonathan Settel. Thrilling to hear, you will enjoy listening to the Hebrew names, expressions and locations as spoken by Messiah.

20 CDs	JC01	$49.99
MP3	JC02	$49.99

Jewish New Testament & Commentary on CD-ROM

Do word searches, studies and more! And, because this is part of the popular LOGOS Bible program, you will have the "engine" to access one of the top Bible research systems. As an option, you'll be able to obtain and cross reference the Mishnah, Josephus, Bible dictionaries, and much more! Windows 3.1+ only.

	JCD02	$39.99

Messianic Judaism *A Modern Movement With an Ancient Past*
—David H. Stern

An updated discussion of the history, ideology, theology and program for Messianic Judaism. A challenge to both Jews and non-Jews who honor Yeshua to catch the vision of Messianic Judaism. 312 pages

	LB62	$17.99

Restoring the Jewishness of the Gospel

A Message for Christians
—David H. Stern

Introduces Christians to the Jewish roots of their faith, challenges some conventional ideas, and raises some neglected questions: How are both the Jews and "the Church" God's people? Is the Law of Moses in force today? Filled with insight! Endorsed by Dr. Darrell L. Bock. 110 pages

English	LB70	$9.99
Spanish	JB14	$9.99

Yeshua *A Guide to the Real Jesus and the Original Church*
—Dr. Ron Moseley

Opens up the history of the Jewish roots of the Christian faith. Illuminates the Jewish background of Yeshua and the Church and never flinches from showing "Jesus was a Jew, who was born, lived, and died, within first century Judaism." Explains idioms in the New Testament. Endorsed by Dr. Brad Young and Dr. Marvin Wilson. 213 pages.

	LB29	$12.99

Matthew Presents Yeshua, King Messiah *A Messianic Commentary*
—Rabbi Barney Kasdan

Few commentators are able to truly present Yeshua in his Jewish context. Most don't understand his background, his family, even his religion, and consequently really don't understand who he truly is. This commentator is well versed with first-century Jewish practices and thought, as well as the historical and cultural setting of the day, and the 'traditions of the Elders' that Yeshua so often spoke about. Get to know Yeshua, the King, through the writing of another rabbi, Barney Kasdan. 448 pages

LB76	$29.99

James the Just Presents Application of Torah

A Messianic Commentary

—Dr. David Friedman

James (Jacob) one of the Epistles written to first century Jewish followers of Yeshua. Dr. David Friedman, a former Professor of the Israel Bible Institute has shed new light for Christians from this very important letter.

978-1936716449	LB82	$14.99

To the Ends of the Earth – How the First Jewish Followers of Yeshua Transformed the Ancient World
— Dr. Jeffery Seif

Everyone knows that the first followers of Yeshua were Jews, and that Christianity was very Jewish for the first 50 to 100 years. It's a known fact that there were many congregations made up mostly of Jews, although the false perception today is, that in the second century they disappeared. Dr. Seif reveals the truth of what happened to them and how these early Messianic Jews influenced and transformed the behavior of the known world at that time.

978-1936716463	LB83	$17.99

Passion for Israel: *A Short History of the Evangelical Church's Support of Israel and the Jewish People*
—Dan Juster

History reveals a special commitment of Christians to the Jews as God's still elect people, but the terrible atrocities committed against the Jews by so-called Christians have overshadowed the many good deeds that have been performed. This important history needs to be told to help heal the wounds and to inspire more Christians to stand together in support of Israel.

978-1936716401	LB78	$9.99

On The Way to Emmaus: *Searching the Messianic Prophecies*
—Dr. Jacques Doukhan

An outstanding compilation of the most critical Messianic prophecies by a renowned conservative Christian Scholar, drawing on material from the Bible, Rabbinic sources, Dead Sea Scrolls, and more.

978-1936716432	LB80	$14.99

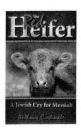

The Red Heifer *A Jewish Cry for Messiah*
—Anthony Cardinale

Award-winning journalist and playwright Anthony Cardinale has traveled extensively in Israel, and recounts here his interviews with Orthodox rabbis, secular Israelis, and Palestinian Arabs about the current search for a red heifer by Jewish radicals wishing to rebuild the Temple and bring the Messiah. These real-life interviews are interwoven within an engaging and dramatic fictional portrayal of the diverse people of Israel and how they would react should that red heifer be found. Readers will find themselves in the Land, where they can hear learned rabbis and ordinary Israelis talking about the red heifer and dealing with all the related issues and the imminent coming and identity of Messiah Yeshua.

| 978-1936716470 | LB79 | $19.99 |

The Return of the Kosher Pig
—Tzahi Shapira

The subject of Messiah fills many pages of Rabbinic writings. Hidden in those pages is a little known concept that the Messiah has the same authority given to God. Based on that concept this book shows the deity of Yeshua from a new perspective. You will see that the rabbis of old expected the Messiah to be deity.

| 978-1936716456 | LB81 | TBD |

Good News According To Matthew
—Dr. Henry Einspruch

English translation with quotations from the Tanakh (Old Testament) capitalized and printed in Hebrew. Helpful notations are included. Lovely black and white illustrations throughout the book. 86 pages.

| | **LB03** | $4.99 |
| Also available in Yiddish. | **LB02** | $4.99 |

The Gospels in their Jewish Context
—John Fischer, Th.D, Ph.D.

An examination of the Jewish background and nature of the Gospels in their contemporary political, cultural and historical settings, emphasizing each gospel's special literary presentation of Yeshua, and highlighting the cultural and religious contexts necessary for understanding each of the gospels. 32 hours of audio/video instruction on MP3-DVD and pdf of syllabus.

| | **LCD01** | $49.99 |

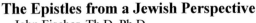

The Epistles from a Jewish Perspective
—John Fischer, Th.D, Ph.D.

An examination of the relationship of Rabbi Shaul (the Apostle Paul) and the Apostles to their Jewish contemporaries and environment; surveys their Jewish practices, teaching, controversy with the religious leaders, and many critical passages, with emphasis on the Jewish nature, content, and background of these letters. 32 hours of audio/video instruction on MP3-DVD and pdf of syllabus.

| | **LCD02** | $49.99 |

Gateways to Torah *Joining the Ancient Conversation on the Weekly Portion*
—Rabbi Russell Resnik

From before the days of Messiah until today, Jewish people have read from and discussed a prescribed portion of the Pentateuch each week. Now, a Messianic Jewish Rabbi, Russell Resnik, brings another perspective on the Torah, that of a Messianic Jew. 246 pages.

LB42	$15.99

Creation to Completion *A Guide to Life's Journey from the Five Books of Moses*
—Rabbi Russell Resnik

Endorsed by Coach Bill McCartney, Founder of Promise Keepers & Road to Jerusalem: "Paul urged Timothy to study the Scriptures (2 Tim. 3:16), advising him to apply its teachings to all aspects of his life. Since there was no New Testament then, this rabbi/apostle was convinced that his disciple would profit from studying the Torah, the Five Books of Moses, and the Old Testament. Now, Rabbi Resnik has written a warm devotional commentary that will help you understand and apply the Law of Moses to your life in a practical way." 256 pages

LB61	$14.99

Walk Genesis! Walk Exodus! Walk Leviticus! Walk Numbers! Walk Deuteronomy!
Messianic Jewish Devotional Commentaries
—Jeffrey Enoch Feinberg, Ph.D.

Using the weekly synagogue readings, Dr. Jeffrey Feinberg has put together some very valuable material in his "Walk" series. Each section includes a short Hebrew lesson (for the non-Hebrew speaker), key concepts, an excellent overview of the portion, and some practical applications. Can be used as a daily devotional as well as a Bible study tool.

Walk Genesis!	238 pages	**LB34**	$12.99
Walk Exodus!	224 pages	**LB40**	$12.99
Walk Leviticus!	208 pages	**LB45**	$12.99
Walk Numbers!	211 pages	**LB48**	$12.99
Walk Deuteronomy!	231 pages	**LB51**	$12.99
SPECIAL! Five-book Walk!	5 Book Set **Save $10**	**LK28**	$54.99

They Loved the Torah *What Yeshua's First Followers Really Thought About the Law*
—Dr. David Friedman
Although many Jews believe that Paul taught against the Law, this book disproves that notion. An excellent case for his premise that all the first followers of the Messiah were not only Torah-observant, but also desired to spread their love for God's entire Word to the gentiles to whom they preached. 144 pages. Endorsed by Dr. David Stern, Ariel Berkowitz, Rabbi Dr. Stuart Dauermann & Dr. John Fischer.
                                    LB47 $9.99

The Distortion *2000 Years of Misrepresenting the Relationship Between Jesus the Messiah and the Jewish People*
—Dr. John Fischer & Dr. Patrice Fischer
Did the Jews kill Jesus? Did they really reject him? With the rise of global anti–Semitism, it is important to understand what the Gospels teach about the relationship between Jewish people and their Messiah. 2000 years of distortion have made this difficult. Learn how the distortion began and continues to this day and what you can do to change it. 126 pages. Endorsed by Dr. Ruth Fleischer, Rabbi Russell Resnik, Dr. Daniel C. Juster, Dr. Michael Rydelnik.
                                    LB54 $11.99

eBooks Now Available!

All books are available as ebooks for your favorite reader

Visit www.messianicjewish.net for direct links to these readers for each available eBook.

God's Appointed Times *A Practical Guide to Understanding and Celebrating the Biblical Holidays* – **New Edition.**

—Rabbi Barney Kasdan

The Biblical Holy Days teach us about the nature of God and his plan for mankind, and can be a source of God's blessing for all believers–Jews and Gentiles–today. Includes historical background, traditional Jewish observance, New Testament relevance, and prophetic significance, plus music, crafts and holiday recipes. 145 pages.

English	**LB63**	$12.99
Spanish	**LB59**	$12.99

God's Appointed Customs *A Messianic Jewish Guide to the Biblical Lifecycle and Lifestyle*

— Rabbi Barney Kasdan

Explains how biblical customs are often the missing key to unlocking the depths of Scripture. Discusses circumcision, the Jewish wedding, and many more customs mentioned in the New Testament. Companion to *God's Appointed Times*. 170 pages.

English	**LB26**	$12.99
Spanish	**LB60**	$12.99

Celebrations of the Bible *A Messianic Children's Curriculum*

Did you know that each Old Testament feast or festival finds its fulfillment in the New? They enrich the lives of people who experience and enjoy them. Our popular curriculum for children is in a brand new, user-friendly format. The lay-flat at binding allows you to easily reproduce handouts and worksheets. Celebrations of the Bible has been used by congregations, Sunday schools, ministries, homeschoolers, and individuals to teach children about the biblical festivals. Each of these holidays are presented for Preschool (2-K), Primary (Grades 1-3), Junior (Grades 4-6), and Children's Worship/Special Services. 208 pages.

LB55 $24.99

Passover: *The Key That Unlocks the Book of Revelation*

—Daniel C. Juster, Th.D.

Is there any more enigmatic book of the Bible than Revelation? Controversy concerning its meaning has surrounded it back to the first century. Today, the arguments continue. Yet, Dan Juster has given us the key that unlocks the entire book—the events and circumstances of the Passover/Exodus. By interpreting Revelation through the lens of Exodus, Dan Juster provides a unified overview that helps us read Revelation as it was always meant to be read, as a drama of spiritual conflict, deliverance, and above all, worship. He also shows how this final drama, fulfilled in Messiah, resonates with the Torah and all of God's Word. — Russ Resnik, Executive Director, Union of Messianic Jewish Congregations.

LB74 $10.99

The Messianic Passover Haggadah

Revised and Updated

—Rabbi Barry Rubin and Steffi Rubin.

Guides you through the traditional Passover seder dinner, step-by-step. Not only does this observance remind us of our rescue from Egyptian bondage, but, we remember Messiah's last supper, a Passover seder. The theme of redemption is seen throughout the evening. What's so unique about our Haggadah is the focus on Yeshua (Jesus) the Messiah and his teaching, especially on his last night in the upper room. 36 pages.

English	**LB57**	$4.99
Spanish	**LBSP01**	$4.99

The Messianic Passover Seder Preparation Guide

Includes recipes, blessings and songs. 19 pages.

English	**LB10**	$2.99
Spanish	**LBSP02**	$2.99

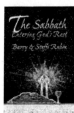

The Sabbath *Entering God's Rest*

—Barry Rubin & Steffi Rubin

Even if you've never celebrated Shabbat before, this book will guide you into the rest God has for all who would enter in—Jews and non-Jews. Contains prayers, music, recipes; in short, everything you need to enjoy the Sabbath, even how to observe havdalah, the closing ceremony of the Sabbath. Also discusses the Saturday or Sunday controversy. 48 pages.

LB32 $6.99

Havdalah *The Ceremony that Completes the Sabbath*

—Dr. Neal & Jamie Lash

The Sabbath ends with this short, yet equally sweet ceremony called havdalah (separation). This ceremony reminds us to be a light and a sweet fragrance in this world of darkness as we carry the peace, rest, joy and love of the Sabbath into the work week. 28 pages.

LB69 $4.99

Dedicate and Celebrate!

A Messianic Jewish Guide to Hanukkah

—Barry Rubin & Family

Hanukkah means "dedication" — a theme of significance for Jews and Christians. Discussing its historical background, its modern-day customs, deep meaning for all of God's people, this little book covers all the how-tos! Recipes, music, and prayers for lighting the menorah, all included! 32 pages.

LB36 $4.99

The Conversation
An Intimate Journal of the Emmaus Encounter
—Judy Salisbury

"Then beginning with Moses and with all the prophets, He explained to them the things concerning Himself in all the Scriptures." Luke 24:27
If you've ever wondered what that conversation must have been like, this captivating book takes you there.
"The Conversation brings to life that famous encounter between the two disciples and our Lord Jesus on the road to Emmaus. While it is based in part on an imaginative reconstruction, it is filled with the throbbing pulse of the excitement of the sensational impact that our Lord's resurrection should have on all of our lives." ~ Dr. Walter Kaiser President Emeritus Gordon-Conwell Theological Seminary. Hardcover 120 pages.
LB73 $14.99

Growing to Maturity
A Messianic Jewish Discipleship Guide
—Daniel C. Juster, Th.D.

This discipleship series presents first steps of understanding and spiritual practice, tailored for the Jewish believer. It's purpose is to aid the believer in living according to Yeshua's will as a disciple, one who has learned the example of his teacher. The course is structured according to recent advances in individualized educational instruction. Discipleship is serious business and the material is geared for serious study and reflection. Each chapter is divided into short sections followed by study questions. 256 pages.
LB75 $19.99

Growing to Maturity Primer: *A Messianic Jewish Discipleship Workbook*
—Daniel C. Juster, Th.D.

A basic book of material in question and answer form. Usable by everyone. 60 pages.
TB16 $7.99

Proverbial Wisdom & Common Sense
—Derek Leman

A Messianic Jewish Approach to Today's Issues from the Proverbs Unique in style and scope, this commentary on the book of Proverbs, written in devotional style, is divided into chapters suitable for daily reading. A virtual encyclopedia of practical advice on family, sex, finances, gossip, honesty, love, humility, and discipline. Endorsed by Dr. John Walton, Dr. Jeffrey Feinberg and Rabbi Barney Kasdan. 248 pages.
LB35 $14.99

That They May Be One *A Brief Review of Church Restoration Movements and Their Connection to the Jewish People*
—Daniel Juster, Th.D

Something prophetic and momentous is happening. The Church is finally fully grasping its relationship to Israel and the Jewish people. Author describes the restoration movements in Church history and how they connected to Israel and the Jewish people. Each one contributed in some way—some more, some less—toward the ultimate unity between Jews and Gentiles. Predicted in the Old Testament and fulfilled in the New, Juster believes this plan of God finds its full expression in Messianic Judaism. He may be right. See what you think as you read *That They May Be One*. 100 pages.

LB71 $9.99

The Greatest Commandment
How the Sh'ma Leads to More Love in Your Life
—Irene Lipson

"What is the greatest commandment?" Yeshua was asked. His reply—"Hear, O Israel, the Lord our God, the Lord is one, and you are to love Adonai your God with all your heart, with all your soul, with all your understanding, and all your strength." A superb book explaining each word so the meaning can be fully grasped and lived. Endorsed by Elliot Klayman, Susan Perlman, & Robert Stearns. 175 pages.

LB65 $12.99

Blessing the King of the Universe
Transforming Your Life Through the Practice of Biblical Praise
—Irene Lipson

Insights into the ancient biblical practice of blessing God are offered clearly and practically. With examples from Scripture and Jewish tradition, this book teaches the biblical formula used by men and women of the Bible, including the Messiah; points to new ways and reasons to praise the Lord; and explains more about the Jewish roots of the faith. Endorsed by Rabbi Barney Kasdan, Dr. Mitch Glaser, & Rabbi Dr. Dan Cohn-Sherbok. 144 pages.

LB53 $11.99

You Bring the Bagels, I'll Bring the Gospel
Sharing the Messiah with Your Jewish Neighbor
Revised Edition—Now with Study Questions
—Rabbi Barry Rubin

This "how-to-witness-to-Jewish-people" book is an orderly presentation of everything you need to share the Messiah with a Jewish friend. Includes Messianic prophecies, Jewish objections to believing, sensitivities in your witness, words to avoid. A "must read" for all who care about the Jewish people. Good for individual or group study. Used in Bible schools. Endorsed by Harold A. Sevener, Dr. Walter C. Kaiser, Dr. Erwin J. Kolb and Dr. Arthur F. Glasser. 253 pages.

English	**LB13**	$12.99
Te Tengo Buenas Noticias	**OBSP02**	$14.99

Making Eye Contact With God
A Weekly Devotional for Women
—Terri Gillespie

What kind of eyes do you have? Are they downcast and sad? Are they full of God's joy and passion? See yourself through the eyes of God. Using real life anecdotes, combined with scripture, the author reveals God's heart for women everywhere, as she softly speaks of the ways in which women see God. Endorsed by prominent authors: Dr. Angela Hunt, Wanda Dyson and Kathryn Mackel. 247 pages, hardcover.

LB68 $19.99

Divine Reversal
The Transforming Ethics of Jesus
—Rabbi Russell Resnik

In the Old Testament, God often reversed the plans of man. Yeshua's ethics continue this theme. Following his path transforms one's life from within, revealing the source of true happiness, forgiveness, reconciliation, fidelity and love. From the introduction, "As a Jewish teacher, Jesus doesn't separate matters of theology from practice. His teaching is consistently practical, ethical, and applicable to real life, even two thousand years after it was originally given." Endorsed by Jonathan Bernis, Dr. Daniel C. Juster, Dr. Jeffrey L. Seif, and Dr Darrell Bock. 206 pages

LB72 $12.99

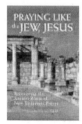

Praying Like the Jew, Jesus
Recovering the Ancient Roots of New Testament Prayer
—Dr. Timothy P. Jones

This eye-opening book reveals the Jewish background of many of Yeshua's prayers. Historical vignettes "transport" you to the times of Yeshua so you can grasp the full meaning of Messiah's prayers. Unique devotional thoughts and meditations, presented in down-to-earth language, provide inspiration for a more meaningful prayer life and help you draw closer to God. Endorsed by Mark Galli, James W. Goll, Rev. Robert Stearns, James F. Strange, and Dr. John Fischer. 144 pages.

LB56 $9.99

Growing Your Olive Tree Marriage *A Guide for Couples from Two Traditions*
—David J. Rudolph

One partner is Jewish; the other is Christian. Do they celebrate Hanukkah, Christmas or both? Do they worship in a church or a synagogue? How will the children be raised? This is the first book from a biblical perspective that addresses the concerns of intermarried couples, offering a godly solution. Includes highlights of interviews with intermarried couples. Endorsed by Walter C. Kaiser, Jr., Rabbi Dan Cohn-Sherbok, Jonathan Settel, Dr. Mitchell Glaser & Natalie Sirota. 224 pages.

LB50 $12.99

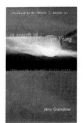

In Search of the Silver Lining *Where is God in the Mids. of Life's Storms?*
—Jerry Gramckow

When faced with suffering, what are your choices? Storms have always raged. And people have either perished in their wake or risen above the tempests, shaping history by their responses…new storms are on the horizon. How will we deal with them? How will we shape history or those who follow us? The answer lies in how we view God in the midst of the storms. Endorsed by Joseph C. Aldrich, Ray Beeson, Dr. Daniel Juster. 176 pages.

LB39 $10.99

The Voice of the Lord *Messianic Jewish Daily Devotional*
—Edited by David J. Rudolph

Brings insight into the Jewish Scriptures—both Old and New Testaments. Twenty-two prominent Messianic contributors provide practical ways to apply biblical truth. Start your day with this unique resource. Explanatory notes. Perfect companion to the Complete Jewish Bible (see page 2). Endorsed by Edith Schaeffer, Dr. Arthur F. Glaser, Dr. Michael L. Brown, Mitch Glaser and Moishe Rosen. 416 pages.

LB31 $19.99

Kingdom Relationships *God's Laws for the Community of Faith*
—Dr. Ron Moseley

Focuses on the teaching of Torah—the Five Books of Moses—tapping into truths that greatly help modern-day members of the community of faith. 64 pages.

LB37 $8.99

His Names Are Wonderful

Getting to Know God Through His Hebrew Names
—Elizabeth L. Vander Meulen and Barbara D. Malda

In Hebrew thought, names did more than identify people; they revealed their nature. God's identity is expressed not in one name, but in many. This book will help readers know God better as they uncover the truths in his Hebrew names. 160 pages.

LB58 $9.99

Train Up A Child *Successful Parenting For The Next Generation*
—Dr. Daniel L. Switzer

The author, former principal of Ets Chaiyim Messianic Jewish Day School, and father of four, combines solid biblical teaching with Jewish sources on child raising, focusing on the biblical holy days, giving fresh insight into fulfilling the role of parent. 188 pages. Endorsed by Dr. David J. Rudolph, Paul Lieberman, and Dr. David H. Stern.

LB64 $12.99

Fire on the Mountain - *Past Renewals, Present Revivals and the Coming Return of Israel*
—Dr. Louis Goldberg

The term "revival" is often used to describe a person or congregation turning to God. Is this something that "just happens," or can it be brought about? Dr. Louis Goldberg, author and former professor of Hebrew and Jewish Studies at Moody Bible Institute, examines real revivals that took place in Bible times and applies them to today. 268 pages.

LB38 $15.99

Voices of Messianic Judaism *Confronting Critical Issues Facing a Maturing Movement*
—General Editor Rabbi Dan Cohn-Sherbok

Many of the best minds of the Messianic Jewish movement contributed their thoughts to this collection of 29 substantive articles. Challenging questions are debated: The involvement of Gentiles in Messianic Judaism? How should outreach be accomplished? Liturgy or not? Intermarriage? 256 pages.

LB46 $15.99

The Enduring Paradox *Exploratory Essays in Messianic Judaism*
—General Editor Dr. John Fischer

Yeshua and his Jewish followers began a new movement—Messianic Judaism—2,000 years ago. In the 20th century, it was reborn. Now, at the beginning of the 21st century, it is maturing. Twelve essays from top contributors to the theology of this vital movement of God, including: Dr. Walter C. Kaiser, Dr. David H. Stern, and Dr. John Fischer. 196 pages.

LB43 $13.99

The World To Come *A Portal to Heaven on Earth*
—Derek Leman

An insightful book, exposing fallacies and false teachings surrounding this extremely important subject... paints a hopeful picture of the future and dispels many non-biblical notions. Intriguing chapters: Magic and Desire, The Vision of the Prophets, Hints of Heaven, Horrors of Hell, The Drama of the Coming Ages. Offers a fresh, but old, perspective on the world to come, as it interacts with the prophets of Israel and the Bible. 110 pages.

LB67   .$9.99

Hebrews Through a Hebrew's Eyes
—Dr. Stuart Sacks

Written to first-century Messianic Jews, this epistle, understood through Jewish eyes, edifies and encourages all. 119 pages. Endorsed by Dr. R.C. Sproul and James M. Boice.

LB23 $10.99

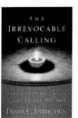

The Irrevocable Calling *Israel's Role As A Light To The Nations*
—Daniel C. Juster, Th.D.

Referring to the chosen-ness of the Jewish people, Paul, the Apostle, wrote "For God's free gifts and his calling are irrevocable" (Rom. 11:29). This messenger to the Gentiles understood the unique calling of his people, Israel. So does Dr. Daniel Juster, President of Tikkun Ministries Int'l. In *The Irrevocable Calling*, he expands Paul's words, showing how Israel was uniquely chosen to bless the world and how these blessings can be enjoyed today. Endorsed by Dr. Jack Hayford, Mike Bickle and Don Finto. 64 pages.

LB66	$8.99

Are There Two Ways of Atonement?
—Dr. Louis Goldberg

Here Dr. Louis Goldberg, long-time professor of Jewish Studies at Moody Bible Institute, exposes the dangerous doctrine of Two-Covenant Theology. 32 pages.

LB12	$ 4.99

Awakening *Articles and Stories About Jews and Yeshua*
—Arranged by Anna Portnov

Articles, testimonies, and stories about Jewish people and their relationship with God, Israel, and the Messiah. Includes the effective tract, "The Most Famous Jew of All." One of our best anthologies for witnessing to Jewish people. Let this book witness for you! Russian version also available. 110 pages.

English	**LB15**	$ 6.99
Russian	**LB14**	$ 6.99

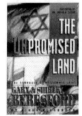

The Unpromised Land *The Struggle of Messianic Jews Gary and Shirley Beresford*
—Linda Alexander

They felt God calling them to live in Israel, the Promised Land. Wanting nothing more than to live quietly and grow old together in the country of refuge for all Jewish people, little did they suspect what events would follow to try their faith. The fight to make *aliyah*, to claim their rightful inheritance in the Promised Land, became a battle waged not only for themselves, but also for Messianic Jews all over the world that wish to return to the Jewish homeland. Here is the true saga of the Beresford's journey to the land of their forefathers. 216 pages.

LB19	$ 9.99

Death of Messiah *Twenty fascinating articles that address a subject of grief, hope, and ultimate triumph.*
—Edited by Kai Kjaer-Hansen

This compilation, written by well-known Jewish believers, addresses the issue of Messiah and offers proof that Yeshua—the true Messiah—not only died, but also was resurrected! 160 pages.

LB20 $ 8.99

Beloved Dissident *(A Novel)*
—Laurel West

A gripping story of human relationships, passionate love, faith, and spiritual testing. Set in the world of high finance, intrigue, and international terrorism, the lives of David, Jonathan, and Leah intermingle on many levels--especially their relationships with one another and with God. As the two men tangle with each other in a rising whirlwind of excitement and danger, each hopes to win the fight for Leah's love. One of these rivals will move Leah to a level of commitment and love she has never imagined--or dared to dream. Whom will she choose? 256 pages.

LB33 $ 9.99

Sudden Terror
—Dr. David Friedman

Exposes the hidden agenda of militant Islam. The author, a former member of the Israel Defense Forces, provides eye-opening information needed in today's dangerous world.

Dr. David Friedman recounts his experiences confronting terrorism; analyzes the biblical roots of the conflict between Israel and Islam; provides an overview of early Islam; demonstrates how the United States and Israel are bound together by a common enemy; and shows how to cope with terrorism and conquer fear. The culmination of many years of research and personal experiences. This expose will prepare you for what's to come! 160 pages.

LB49 $ 9.99

It is Good! *Growing Up in a Messianic Family*
—Steffi Rubin

Growing up in a Messianic Jewish family. Meet Tovah! Tovah (Hebrew for "Good") is growing up in a Messianic Jewish home, learning the meaning of God's special days. Ideal for young children, it teaches the biblical holidays and celebrates faith in Yeshua. 32 pages to read & color.

LB11 $ 4.99

These books, by the founders of our organization, were some of the first books of their kind, ever. They were instrumental in bringing many Jewish people to faith in Yeshua and helped launch Messianic Jewish Publishers and the Messianic Jewish movement.

A Way In The Wilderness *Essays in Messianic Jewish Thought*
—M.G. Einspruch

Did the Jews kill Jesus? Is the New Testament anti-Semitic? Immortality in Jewish thought. What is a Jew? These are just a few of the topics addressed. Written by well-known Jewish believers in the Messiah--Victor Buksbazen, Daniel Fuchs, Henry Einspruch, and more. Thousands of copies of this book have been shared with seekers around the world. Includes a chapter on Messianic prophecy. A classic and valuable resource! "Excellent. One cannot improve upon it." --*the late Messianic Jewish scholar, Rachmiel Frydland* 112 pages.

| LB04 | $ 7.99 |

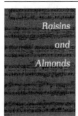

Raisins And Almonds
—edited by Henry & Marie Einspruch

Poetry, testimonies, music, photographs, illustrations, brief essays and points to ponder. Edited by Henry and Marie Einspruch, this little book has been shared with thousands around the globe! Now it's your turn to pass it on to your Jewish friends. 87 pages.

| LB05 | $ 5.99 |

The Ox, The Ass, The Oyster
—edited by Henry & Marie Einspruch

A collection of articles and stories originally presented over the radio in Yiddish (now in English). This book is presented in the hope that it will challenge the reader to compare the mundane, materialistic things of everyday life, with the world of truth, justice, love, judgment, and forgiveness. 100 pages.

| LB06 | $ 5.99 |

Would I, Would You?
—edited by Henry & Marie Einspruch

Here are the stories of 14 Jewish people who became believers in Yeshua, including an Orthodox rabbi! Includes the 53rd chapter of Isaiah in Hebrew and Yiddish. Another little gem that has been distributed to thousands around the world. 95 pages.

| LB07 | $ 5.99 |

The Man With The Book
The life and testimony of Henry Einspruch, translator of the Yiddish New Testament and founder of The Lederer Foundation, the parent company of Messianic Jewish Publishers and Resources. 20 pages.

| LB08 | $ 2.99 |